T0026701

The Age *of* PHILLIS

WESLEYAN POETRY

The Age *of*

Phillis

HONORÉE FANONNE JEFFERS

WESLEYAN UNIVERSITY PRESS

Middletown, Connecticut

Wesleyan University Press
Middletown CT 06459
www.wesleyan.edu/wespress
Copyright © 2020 Honorée Fanonne Jeffers. All rights reserved.
Manufactured in the United States of America
First paperback edition 2022
Paperback ISBN 978-0-8195-7950-8
Designed by Richard Hendel
Typeset in Galliard by Passumpsic Publishing
5 4 3 2 1

The Library of Congress cataloged the hardcover edition as:
NAMES: Jeffers, Honorée Fanonne, 1967– author.
TITLE: The age of Phillis / Honorée Fanonne Jeffers.
DESCRIPTION: Middletown: Wesleyan University Press,
    2020. | Series: Wesleyan poetry | Includes bibliographical
    references. | Summary: "A collection of original poems speaking
    to the life and times of Phillis Wheatley, a Colonial America-era
    poet brought to Boston as a slave"—Provided by publisher.
IDENTIFIERS: LCCN 2019040204 (print) | LCCN 2019040205 (ebook) |
    ISBN 9780819579492 (cloth) | ISBN 9780819579515 (ebook)
SUBJECTS: LCSH: Wheatley, Phillis, 1753–1784—Poetry. | African American
    women authors—Poetry. | Women slaves—Massachusetts—Boston
    —Poetry. | Slavery—Massachusetts—History—18th century—
    Poetry. | LCGFT: Poetry.
CLASSIFICATION: LCC PS3560.E365 A74 2020 (print) | LCC PS3560.E365
    (ebook) | DDC 811/.54—dc23
LC record available at https://lccn.loc.gov/2019040204
LC ebook record available at https://lccn.loc.gov/2019040205

for Phillis Wheatley Peters

CONTENTS

Prologue: Mother/Muse

This is a song for the genius child.
Sing it softly, for the song is wild.
— Langston Hughes, from "Genius Child"

....

Mercy, girl.
What the mother might have said, pointing

at the sun rising, what makes life possible.
Then, dripped the bowl of water,

reverent, into oblivious earth.
Was this prayer for her?

Respect for the dead or disappeared?
An act to please *a genius child*?

Her daughter would speak
of water, bowl, sun—

light arriving,
light gone—

sometime after the nice white lady
paid and named her for the slave ship.

Mercy: what the child called Phillis
would claim after that sea journey.

Journey.
Let's call it that.

Let's lie to each other.

Not early descent into madness.
Naked travail among filth and rats.

What got Phillis over that sea?
What kept a stolen daughter?

Perhaps it was *mercy*,
Dear Reader.

Mercy,
Dear Brethren.

Water, bowl, sun—
a mothering, God's milky sound.

Morning shards, and a mother wondered
if her daughter forgot her real name,

refused to envision the rest:
baby teeth missing

and somebody wrapping her treasure
(barely) in a dirty carpet.

'Twas mercy.
You know the story—

how we've lied to each other.

Book: Before

And pleasing Gambia on my soul returns,
With native grace in Spring's luxuriant reign,
Smiles the gay mead and Eden blooms again,
The various bower, the tuneful flowing stream,
The soft retreats, the lovers golden dream . . .
— Phillis Wheatley, from "PHILIS's Reply to the Answer
   in our Last by the Gentleman in the Navy"

What is Africa to me:
Copper sun or scarlet sea,
Jungle star or jungle track,
Strong bronzed men, or regal black
Women from whose loins I sprang
When the birds of Eden sang?
— Countee Cullen, from "Heritage"

c. Sometime in antiquity, date unknown

Utilitarian—
        then,
                at some point,
                        an embrace of beauty.
        A glow:
        the man waits,
a picture in his head.
        He will claw
                out the dream's
                        tincture,
                pour it into mold—
        and in that dream,
he has met
        the hyena laughing
                about chains. The man
                        will pound metal
                to forget that
        grievous sound.
He will master
        what was brought
                from earth,
                        from viscera's
                need—
        until his hands seize,
he will do this work,
        and his son will do
                the same,
                        and it will be written
                upon the griot's skull.

MOTHERING #1

Yaay, Someplace in the Gambia, c. 1753

after
the after-birth
is delivered
the mother stops
holding her breath
the mid-wife gives
what came before
her just-washed pain
her insanity pain
an undeserved pain
a God-given pain
oh oh oh pain
drum-talking pain
witnessing pain
Allah
a mother offers
You this gift
prays You find
it acceptable
her living pain
her creature pain
her pretty-little-baby
pain

FATHERING #1

Baay, Someplace in the Gambia, c. 1753

After the required time,
the seclusion to fool scream-faced
souls: the naming ceremony.
People arrive with gifts
for the close-eyed baby with no sense,
separate into men and women.
They do not count their children
like bad-lucked livestock—
they eat. They talk.
Chew kola.
Pray at the required
times. Then: eat.
Still: eat.
The baby unaware of her meaning.
In years, her father's expectation:
her body hailing a good
bride price, that she might
sing forth sons—
if she prays as well.
At any rate, boys clearly hear
the loudest greeting.
Births to be cherished.
Tribal hierarchy.
God. (Him only or grouped,
translated stars.)
A man. His wife.
(Maybe: two more.)
A girl sits right at the bottom—
and yet,
her father carries her high.
With this bone-gourd,
he has become
someone.

DAFA RAFET

Yaay, Baay, and Goonay, Someplace in the Gambia, c. 1756

When mother and child
walk from the village
to gather fruit, faces
recite quotidian love.
        Do you have peace
        (Waw, waw, diam rek)
Then, they are alone, and the toddler
points out the fat-bottomed
baobab, the mango
with its frustrating reach.
Mother pierces a low-hanging
jewel, and her small
shadow trills gratitude.
        Yaay, you are so nice
        (Waw, waw)
        Yaay, I love you so
        (Waw, waw)
No demonstration, but a hand
touching the tender head
that was braided over cries.
Later that night,
the father must listen, too.
        Baay, I ate a mango
        (Waw, waw)
        Baay, I saw a bug
        (Waw, waw)
The child sits closer
to his mat,
whispers ambiguous lights:
        I know all the things—
and he does not answer,
but smiles at his wife:
their daughter is a marvel
and they must pray for humility.

FIRST-TIME PRAYER

Yaay and Goonay, Someplace in the Gambia, c. 1759

The water was preparation.
When the mother
and her child rose
in the morning, no Jesus.
The same God, yet
with ninety-nine monikers.
   We have awoken
   and all of creation
   has awoken, for Allah,
   Lord of all the worlds
The bowl—
wooden or gourd—
was light, as water
and faith are heavy.
In the century after
this mother and child
are dead, someone
will write about
these mornings,
that the mother
poured a ritual
for her daughter
to remember.
This writing someone
won't know of ablutions,
of giving peace,
of purity required
before submission,
that God's servants
had ached
all night to be clean.

....

Someplace in the Gambia, c. 1759

Mystery is the word for my purposes here. This child
frail, not quite whole. Not the leader of the gang. The strange
understanding

to be revealed. Is she dancing with the others?
Is there a shaking of tail feathers, a nonsense ditty? *Shimmy to
the west   Shimmy to the east*

Shake it   Shake it   Shake it   Yeah   Yeah   Yeah
A sharing of secrets with a lagging friend? I'm full of questions.
I can ask History what I want.

I can forget the rest. Why will the slave raiders snatch
a thin, sickly girl? Why not leave her behind for the usual spoils?
The men with clubs.

The charcoaled village. The old ones. The babies—
I can say, *No. We won't speak about all that.* I can keep
returning to this blank

someplace before her taking. The story of the red cloth
not yet laid out. *A genius child* playing, brightness in
a mother's crown.

A pearl if she lives by the sea. The strand of a gathered
plait. Needed point: surely, love doesn't rest in emptied air
without some disappointment,

but this is a good moment. Isn't it?—I can run to my own
playground, remember a cupped palm next to my ear. I can call
my mother who is yet alive.

I can claim my memories. She can answer her ringing
telephone. I won't forget her name or mine.

FRACTURE

West Africa, c. 15th century to 19th century

The men arrive. Slave ships are anchored.
The men arrive. The traders gather.
The men arrive. The traders march.
The men arrive. The war is waged.
The men arrive. The fire comes.
The men arrive. The people run.
The men arrive. The chase begins.
The men arrive. The dead abandoned.
The men arrive. The iron sounds.
The men arrive. The people march.
The men arrive. The sea. The sea.
The men arrive. The traders haggle.
The men arrive. The silver laughs.
The men arrive. The castle groans.
The men arrive. The door opens.
The men arrive. The water welcomes.
The men arrive. The mourning longs.
The men arrive. Our names shall scatter.

Someplace/Someplace/Someplace, c. 1761

                                         oh: a war

I have touched my belly
in expectancy, strummed

                                         oh: the family stolen

meat-covered ribs.
The navel's planetary cavern.

                                         oh: slaves already

The thump behind my ear,
talking of cleared ashes.

                                         oh: the lowly caste

Where is my wife?
Where is my daughter?

                                         oh: perhaps a master

I beat my shameful forehead.
I wanted a boy, hard

                                         oh: benevolent tyrant

foot walking me forward.
A boy, then, a man,

                                         oh: does it matter

I thought I preferred—
and here I am, gripping

                                         oh: the family sold

the phantom skirts
of women.

                                         oh: oh oh oh

Where is my wife?
Where is my daughter?

ENTREATY: YAAY

Someplace/Someplace/Someplace, c. 1761

PHILLIS was brought
from Africa to America

                                    small creature spinning

in the Year 1761

                                    my hands reaching

between Seven and Eight
Years of Age
Without any Assistance

                                    still my child

from School Education
and by only what she
was taught in the Family

                                    mine
                                    and don't forget me
                                    or this piece of land
                                    oh come back

attained the English
language to which she
was an utter Stranger
before

                                    my sweet girl
                                    please don't leave

to the great Astonishment
of all who heard her

                                    touch my hands
                                    walk to my side

This Relation is given
by her Master who bought her
JOHN WHEATLEY
Boston

                                    my rare seed   Yaay is calling
                                    come to me

....

The Transatlantic Journey of Goonay, c. Summer 1761

Peas mashed with possibly
tainted fish   A daily pint of water
No   blankets   mother   father
clothes   underwear   dance of modesty

Why the threats of diphtheria   tetanus
malaria   smallpox   diarrhea   dehydration
common cold   diseases   rape

Why the screaming of the grown shelf mates
a woman or two giving birth   Newborns kept
by sailors or capriciously tossed to sharks
Why the banquet of placenta left for rats

The shackled   the crowded   begging to be killed
Why germs and tribes rechristened *Negro*
chattering below   Vomit

Why no bleach   Why no soap to clean
the effluvia of prayer   Why did she survive
asthma and fear on that journey   Why didn't
the ring in her nose get infected

Why did she have to sleep marinating
in her own shit and piss   Why not death
in the middle of this   Why did this child survive

Lord   Lord have *mercy*

FOUND POEM: DETENTION #1

Isaac Chotiner interviewing Warren Binford for the New Yorker, *June 22, 2019*

Question:
> How many kids are
> > at the [detention] facility
> > [in Clint, Texas] right now,
> and do you have some sense
> > of a breakdown of where
> > > they're from?

Answer:
> . . . We were so shocked
> > by the number of children
> who were there, because
> it's a facility that only has capacity
> > for a hundred and four.
> > > And we were told
> > that they had recently
> expanded the facility,
> > but they did not give
> > > us a tour of it,
> > and we legally don't have
> the right to tour the facility.
> > We drove around afterward,
> > > and we discovered that there
> > was a giant warehouse that
> they had put on the site.
> > And it appears
> > > that that one warehouse
> > has allegedly increased
> their capacity by an additional
> > five hundred kids.
> > > When we talked
> > to Border Patrol agents

later that week,
  they confirmed
    that is the alleged expansion,
  and when we talked to children,
one of the children described
  as many as three hundred
    children being in that room,
  in that warehouse,
basically, at one point
  when he first arrived.
    There were no windows.
  And so
what we did then
  was we looked at the ages
    of the children,
  and we were shocked
by just how many
  young children there were.
    There were over a hundred
  young children when we first arrived.
And there were child-mothers
  who were also there,
    and so
  we started to pull
the child-mothers and their babies,
  we started to make sure
    their needs were being met.
  We started to pull
the youngest children
  to see who was taking care of them.
    And then we started
  to pull the children who

had been there the longest
        to find out just how long
                children are being kept there.
        Children described to us
that they've been there
        for three weeks or longer.
           And so,
        immediately from that population
that we were trying to triage,
        they were filthy dirty,
             there was mucus
        on their shirts,
the shirts were dirty.
        We saw breast milk
           on the shirts.
        There was food on the shirts,
and the pants as well.
        They told us
           that they were hungry.
        they told us
that some of them
        had not showered
           or had not showered
        until the day or two days
before we arrived.
        Many of them described
           that they only brushed
        their teeth once.

Book: Passage

You having the command of my Brigg Phillis your Orders
are to Imbrace the first favourable opportunity of Wind &
Weather to proceed to the Coast of Aff-ica—Touching first
at Sinagall . . . Now in Regard to your purchasing Slaves,
you'l Observe to get as few Girl Slaves as PoSsible &
as many Prime Boys as you Can . . .
— Letter from Timothy Fitch to Captain Peter Gwin,
     November 8, 1760

Middle Passage:
          voyage through death
                    to life upon these shores.
— Robert Hayden, from "Middle Passage"

BLUES: ODYSSEUS

How many sat underwater,
entangled by myth's past tense,
before Neptune first raised his
beard in the direction of Ethiopia,
and after, Odysseus—
always living—
was saved by Homer's tablet?
Centuries after that story was written,
in the land of Not Make Believe,
a crew of slave-ship sailors
threw one hundred and thirty-two
Africans into the Atlantic Ocean.
Heave-ho to souls.
And people. And laws. And kin.
But Odysseus lives. He always will,
Our Great White Hope—
before whiteness was invented—
this hero who longs for the wood's sway.
Despite his tendency to chase tail—
sirens and sundry other
poppycock-drinking girls—
I want to be happy that Homer imagined
a sea housing pretty, forgiving Nymphs—
while somewhere else, a wheel dances
and someone else drowns.
Sharks should pass Odysseus by,
never imagining his taste.
The gods shouldn't pull at his fate—
now angry, now benevolent.
I try hard not to blame that man:
We all deserve our Maker's love.

POINT OF NO RETURN

....

Somewhere on the Windward Coast, West Africa c. 1761

[keep the men from muttering among themselves]

parsing the air's dying scent   the water   arms clutching

at mirthful spirit   back to this   bereft lexicon

dante's castle on the rocky isle

captured bodies twirled around the obscene

& what cannot be released is that loud kindred laugh

humanity split along colonial charms   *[virgin girls*

in one cell   do what you wish]   double back to naming

gris-gris town-crying in hell   place your hands on the bone

map of fifteen million   *[women with fallen breasts in another]*

trapped in a century's enlightened whims

forgive these men of three centuries ago   according

to the tenets of baptized slave ships   forgive   forgive

or do not   *[no children   unless that is your taste]*

THE TRANSATLANTIC PROGRESS OF SUGAR
IN THE EIGHTEENTH CENTURY

....

I own I am shock'd at the purchase of slaves,
And fear those who buy them and sell them are knaves . . .
I pity them greatly, but I must be mum,
For how could we do without sugar and rum?
— William Cowper, from "Pity for Poor Africans"

oh
peerless
smell of cane
cloud on triangular
horizon whip trilling a red
aria molasses the smelling hull
& chained bones the practical sharks
trailing hoping for new bodies overboard

(dark/
dark/pale/
dark/pale/dark/
dark/exchange/fresh/
exchange/flesh/exchange/
fresh/blood/blood/blood/blood/
dark/dark/pale/dark/pale/dark/exchange/
flesh/exchange/fresh/exchange/flesh/blood)

&
the sea
taste blessed rape
hollowed burn & brand
some girls mostly boys this holy
trinity of *"godless dirty savages"* island
patois rum down a throat lump in some tea
science of journey & the peerless smell of cane

ILLUSTRATION: "STOWAGE OF THE BRITISH SLAVE SHIP 'BROOKES' UNDER THE REGULATED SLAVE TRADE ACT OF 1788"

There is no air.

Closer. The stinky aria.
    The bodies' relentless outlines

on either side.
    Above, below—

at some distance, the appearance
    of Kente's intricate bands, or,

a longed-for version of what
    a village potter might throw.

I dream of breath,
    the stealing from

pretty faces, the smoothness
    of the best chocolate.

A tweakable, selfish nose.
    A body is *some* body. (I know that.)

And theft?
    The hoping for the death

of somebody else.
    Not of my family.

Not of my tribe.

    My Maker up there,
please, make the one

    next to me die. There is no air.
Give me a teaspoon of life.

I don't care how.

    I don't.

ACCORDING TO THE TESTIMONY TO THE GRAND
JURY OF NEWPORT, RHODE ISLAND, BY SAILORS
JONATHAN CRANSTON AND THOMAS GORTON,
AFTER THROWING A NEGRO WOMAN (REFERRED TO
AS "WENCH") ALIVE INTO THE SEA, JAMES DEWOLF,
CAPTAIN OF THE SLAVE SHIP *POLLY*, MOURNED THE
LOSS OF THE GOOD CHAIR TO WHICH HE HAD
STRAPPED HIS VICTIM

c. June 15, 1791

First Question:

Was it a ball and claw with an embroidered seat
[mercy] that brought on the captain's grief, and not
a common stool, or a slat back, arched or straight,
the high exaggeration, or a Windsor, which is interesting,
too, as the slender rods keep the spine from leaning
far away from the center of gravity, a force that had been
discovered a mere century and a half before, an infant next
to the trade plied by this rich man who would grow
richer and stay free *[mercy]* and find something as precious
as sweet water next to endless salt that made him
mourn the loss of the craftsman's whistle, that moved him
in his duty—and was he afraid, for had Smallpox run
through his crew, the inevitability of insurrection *[mercy]*—
forced him to touch the wood's brown skin one last
time *[mercy]* and pray for the sap's essence soured next
to the assumed-to-be-but-not-proven diseased
Negro wench strapped to it, blindfolded and gagged
[mercy], to inhale the stinking combination, a defilement
of such delicate embroidery, brocade stained, the waste *[mercy]*—
is that what made him throw so good a piece
of furniture into the sea, and watch the sharks take
her into their mouths?

Second Question:

Was that beautiful chair walnut or cherry
and were there carvings along the arms
and legs as well?

CATALOG: WATER

The Zong, 1781–1783

I know I'll try your patience,
as I have for several years:
When I talk of slavery,
you're going to sigh

        impatiently: *Not*
        this black woman again.
        And I'm going to ask,
        do you go to church?

                In the Bible, there's nothing
                that curses the holding of slaves—
                or *servants* as they are
                euphemistically named.

There are displays:
men with no say-so,
eunuchs casually cut,
children forced to play

        with others, hoping mates
        don't fall down
        and hurt themselves,
        lest their slaves be blamed—

                women whose bodies
                are given to their masters,
                loam for foretold seed.
                Slavery's in Genesis,

Leviticus, Deuteronomy,
Matthew, Ephesians,
Colossians, Timothy,
and Peter—

and slavery's in the U. S.
Constitution, and in homes
of Presidents: Washington,
Jefferson, Madison, Monroe,

        Jackson, Tyler,
        Taylor, and Polk—
        slaves work for us *now*
        but I won't upset you

by talking about *new* slavery—
what we eat and use today—
I'll simply pull you
back three centuries

        to prophets blessing slave
        ships in God's mighty name,
        to a trade for African
        merchants not yet

                collected into one tribe—
                not yet *Negro* or *black*,
                but members of separate villages,
                babel dust stuck to the sides

of towers. Racial solidarity
was not yet a thing—
but discussing *African* slave
trading might complicate your

        need for an easy story—
        and so, there once was
        a *European* ship called *The Zong*,
        purchased by a syndicate,

a white legacy
of fathers and sons,
wealthy, sanguine heirs
of patrilineal times.

The Zong sailed down
the side of West Africa,
where ships' captains thought
the land spoke to them:

We will gift you our insides.
There were structures with slaves
in dungeons and whites
in clean quarters above—

the castles, the forts,
the factories that dotted
the coasts: Saint-Louis, Gorée,
Iles de Los, Cape Mount,

Sestos, Grand Bassam,
Axim, Cape Three Points.
The Zong stopped at
Cape Coast, then

Anomaboe and Sao Tomé,
named for the doubting
man to whom Jesus
revealed himself.

The Zong took on four
hundred and forty-two
captives, a tight pack,
and by the time

the ship left for open
water, sixty-two
of those Africans had died.
The vessel's doctor

       would speak of the *bloody*
       flux of the bowels.
       It wasn't his fault
       that a godly act crawled

              through the mouth and down,
              but the doctor was unclear
              about the sadness
              taking over the cargo.

Despair was a deity
calling for tribute, and ships
would give this sad praise:
the *Adventurer*, the *Africa*,

       the *Black Joke*, the *City of London*,
       the *Eagle*, the *Elizabeth*,
       the *Greyhound*, the *Hawk*,
       the *Industrious Bee*,

              the *Nancy*, the *Polly*,
              the *New Britannia*,
              the *Thomas*, the *Triumph*,
              the *True Blue Unity*.

The Zong sailed West, and some
say, one hundred
thirty-two of the enslaved
were *disposed of*.

And some say, one hundred
fifty were *disposed of.*
And some say, one hundred
eighty were *disposed of,*

       that in the night,
       the ship's crew pushed Africans
       through a window, because drinking
       water was running too low.

The sailors kept on the chains
and the Africans quickly sank
into water. The killing took
three days—

       back in Liverpool, the owners
       of *The Zong* were dismayed
       when news of their lost *cargo*
       found them in that city

       of coffeehouses,
       theatres, libraries,
       a ladies' walk, and naturally,
       slave trading.

The owners were seized
by an idea: they decided to sue
their insurance company.
They wanted to be *reimbursed*

       for the value of the chained,
       African dead: there was a trial,
       and then, another,
       and the truth finally

wagged its song:
on the night of the second day
that the crew of *The Zong*
pushed Africans into the sea,

a heavy rain had fallen.
There was no shortage
of water,
not anymore,

but even so,
the crew of *The Zong*
drowned a third batch
of Africans, and then,

the ship sailed on its way.
That's all.
The ship sailed on its way.
No prayers.

The ship sailed on its way.
No funerals.
The ship sailed on its way.—
Here is where I leave

those sailors and owners,
and you can forget
about a happy ending.
I know you want one,

twenty-first-century-style.
A soundtrack. Some ruffled
costumes. An uprising,
since there were plenty

of those, the cutting
open of white sailors
and captains of ships,
such as the mutinies

       on the *Henry*, the *Neptunis*,
       the *Ferris Galley*, the *Brome*,
       the *Meeriman*, the *Little George*,
       the *Hope*, the *William*, the *Felicity*,

              the *Thames*, the *Mary*,
              and the *Jolly Bachelor*—
              but this did not happen
              aboard *The Zong* when

the murder of Africans
began: the last group
of victims leapt overboard
to their death, when they knew

       what was coming—
       and whether the owners
       lost their insurance
       case or won, the Africans

              of *The Zong* drank salt
              at the bottom of the ocean,
              and millions of others
              were enslaved.

How can anything
erase that choking?
Water and time cannot
bury *The Zong*, and neither

can a moving picture.
My sleep is haunted
by chains and catalogs,
and I don't give one damn

        if you grow tired of hearing
        about slavery.
        I will curse sailors and
        their willful, seafaring tales.

Celebrations of Poseidon
throwing tridents.
His bare, pale chest:
wet dream of the canon—

        I'll chant of murder
        trailing through my nightmares,
        so that blood splashes
        when Spirits strut.

        Don't you know that
        drowned folks will rise
        to croon signs to me?
        And anyway, I didn't tell

this story to please you.
I built this altar for them.

FOUND POEM: DETENTION #2

Michael Brice-Saddler, reporting for the Washington Post, *December 15, 2018*

The 7-year-old
    Guatemalan girl
        who died in U.S.
    Border Patrol
custody was healthy
    before she arrived,
        and her family is now
    calling for an
"objective
    and thorough"
        investigation
    into her death,
a representative
    for the family
        said Saturday.
    In a statement,
the family's attorneys
    disputed reports
        that the girl,
    Jakelin Caal,
went several
    days without
        food and water
    before crossing
the border,
    which contradicts
        statements
    by the Department
of Homeland
    Security.
        . . . Jakelin's death
    was announced

Thursday by U.S.
    Customs and
        Border Protection
    after inquiries by the
Washington Post,
    raising questions
        about the conditions
    of their facilities . . .
CBP and Department
    of Homeland Security
        officials deny
    that the agency
is responsible
    for what
        happened
    to the girl.
The Trump
    Administration
        has also denied
    responsibility
for her death.

Book: After

TO BE SOLD
A parcel of likely Negroes imported from *Africa*,
Cheap for Cash, or Credit with Interest; enquire
of *John Avery* at his House, next Door to the white
Horse, or at the Store adjoining to said *Avery's* Distill
House, at the South End, near the South Market:—Also
if any Persons have any Negroe Men, strong and hearty,
tho' not of the best moral Character, which are proper
Subjects for Transportation, may have an Exchange
for small Negroes.
— *Boston-Gazette and Country Journal*, August 3, 1761

Father of mercy, 'twas thy gracious hand
Brought me in safety from those dark abodes.
— Phillis Wheatley, from "To the University of Cambridge,
    in New-England"

Nine years kept secret in the dark abode,
Secure I lay, conceal'd from man and God:
Deep in a cavern'd rock my days were led;
The rushing ocean murmur'd o'er my head.
— from Homer's *The Iliad*, translated by Alexander Pope

MOTHERING #2

Susannah Wheatley, Boston Harbor, Summer 1761

And so,
because the little girl was bony and frail,
Mistress Wheatley gained her for a *trifling*,
passing by the other slaves from the brig called *Phillis*.
The white woman's mind muddled
by what the light revealed: a seven-year-old,
naked, dark body, there for every sailor
to lay his shameless eyes upon,
a child the age of her dead little girl—
I'm trying to both see and discard that day,
as when I stood over the open casket
of an old man, counting the lines on his face,
grieving yet perverse, refusing to believe that hours
from then, he'd be cranked down into the grave—
and so,
the lady tarried in front of the sickly child,
distracted by the gulls screaming at port,
their shadows dogging the constant sea.
They were drawn by the stink of a slave ship,
by lice in unwashed heads of hair,
and so,
she bought that child,
not someone older with muscles—
strong enough to carry a servant's burden.
That was the moment, a humming, epic page.
That one—
in the carriage, a mothering
gesture, finger beneath a chin,
lifting the face up to trust.
The fickle air between them almost love.

She took the child into her home,
fed and bathed her, deciphered
the naps on her head.
Dressed her in strange garments:
gratitude and slavery.
And so.

FATHERING #2

John Wheatley, Boston Harbor, Summer 1761

Or was it the husband who purchased
the little girl? I've thought on this for many
years: how might a wife, a respectable,
white lady, go down to the docks
and complete a fleshy transaction?
What insults might the sailors slide
through her bonnet and modest dress?
She was a mother already.
The still-living twins, Nathaniel
and Mary, salted honey in her older change.
But three earlier children had died:
John (the younger), Susannah (another),
Sarah (gone at the same age as this skinny, dark one)—
their father thought the child might sneak
away his wife's lingering blues.
Was he tender, touching a sparrowed shoulder?
I mean you no harm, child. I give you my vow.
There is a good meal waiting for us at home.
Or was he gruff with a disembarked stranger
as she halted through language she might
have learned on the ship?
And did the child flinch, a foundling
arrived in an altered world?
Too wise when she tasted
the last of verdancy—
understanding that she was naked,
that heroes strip leaves from the trees
they own?

DESK OF MARY WHEATLEY, WHERE SHE MIGHT HAVE TAUGHT THE CHILD (RE)NAMED PHILLIS TO READ

c. Winter 1763

The dark wood no match
for the gorgeous ebony
of the child who leans against it,
while a taller girl teaches
her artful curves and symbols,
the power of letters arranged in a row.
Easy, the ABCs, then short words,
but counting is different.
      In Phillis's home, the Wolof
number in groups of five, but
only possessions or livestock.
It is a bad luck proposition
to count your offspring: you might
as well prepare their funeral winding—
but facile, the learning of English.
The sound of it, then reading.
      When Mary marries the Reverend,
this desk will go with her,
but that is for later.
In this room, she's a maiden,
covered by the name of her father
who is away trading in dry
goods and one or two slaves.
The mother sits in a cushioned
chair, looking up from her sewing
at the two girls,
the oldest pointing at the page,
the baby rounding her mouth.

There is compassion in dust and sun.
If Susannah tilts her head,
she can deceive herself
that another daughter
is quick from the grave,
that Sarah is the girl who laughs.
Anyone can rise from the dead,
for isn't Phillis here and breathing,
and wasn't her ship a coffin?

LOST LETTER #1: PHILLIS WHEATLEY, BOSTON, TO SUSANNAH WHEATLEY, BOSTON

January 18, 1764

Dear Mistress:

Odysseus sailed the ocean like me
and Nymphs held him in their arms.
They are ladies like my yaay.

*[i will burn this letter in the hearth you are
watching me as i smile i am a good girl i am]*

I shall practice my lessons for you
and Miss Mary, pretend Master Nathaniel

does not yank my hair and tell me,
he'll take a razor and shave me bald.
For you, God will scrub my skin—

but when might I see my yaay? I cannot
recall how she would say *bird* or *baby*

or *potato* in that other place.
Yaay needs to see that my teeth grew in,
that I am alive after my long journey.

*[yaay come for me please i shall be a good
girl i have forgotten how to be naughty]*

Today snow comes down. Outside,
a soul has slipped and fallen on the ice.
That's what that crying means.

Your servant and child,
Phillis

PHILLIS WHEATLEY PERUSES VOLUMES OF
THE CLASSICS BELONGING TO HER NEIGHBOR,
THE REVEREND MATHER BYLES

c. 1765

I hope that the days Phillis walked
across the street or around the corner
to explore the reverend's library,
she was escorted by Mary or Susannah.
      We know she was brilliant, this child.
Also: biddable, quiet, no wild tendencies—
a surprise to the learned man,
as she refused to surrender
      the ring through her nose—
so strange—
and he had other expectations
of her Nation, based upon his studies
      of the early (translated)
accounts of her continent, written
by Arabs, Portuguese, and later,
investors of the Royal African Company.
      The reverend might
have quizzed the child on the philosopher
Terence, born in Tunisia, who put
aside alien surprise.
      Motes suspended in the room,
specks of Homer's stories—
as rendered by the (cranky) Pope—
how Odysseus, reckless,
      bobbed around the world.
His sailors, the equally silly crew,
trapped by his urging words
(but not shackles) accompanied him—

       if alone with the Reverend,
I hope there was no danger
for Phillis in his house, that
he and she sat with decent
       space between them.
That he didn't settle her on his lap.
That she didn't want to—
but couldn't—
       slap at his searching fingers.
I hope he was a gentleman.
Book in hand.
Absent, scholar's gaze.

LOST LETTER #2: PHILLIS WHEATLEY, BOSTON, TO SAMSON OCCOM, LONDON

March 10, 1766

Dear Most Reverend Sir:

In the name of our Benevolent Savior
Jesus Christ, I bring you tall greetings.
I have never sat with an Indian before.

*[i write as i am instructed the white
lady's hand patting my shoulder]*

My mistress says your people are savages,
that I should pray for your tarnished souls.
She says that once I was a savage, too.

*[i hurt for my yaay and baay and oh
the mornings of ablutions and millet]*

Mistress says that beasts in my homeland
might have devoured me, before God's *mercy*—
I enclose my unworthy verse,

and I pray for your heathen brethren.
Prayer makes my mistress very happy.

*[the white lady tells me i am lucky
i was saved from my parents
who prayed to carvings and beads*

*she says my yaay and baay are pagans
though i am allowed to keep loving them*

*do you pray for your playmates are they yet
alive i do not know where mine were taken
on that day i am reminded to forget]*

Your humble servant,
Phillis

LOST LETTER #3: SAMSON OCCOM, LONDON, TO PHILLIS WHEATLEY, BOSTON

August 24, 1766

Dear Little Miss Phillis:

I was happy to receive the kind
favors of your letter and poem,
across this wide water that God created.

*[child you are no more savage than me
and what i am is a hungry prayer]*

I teach my young ones from Exodus,
that God can be an angry man
and vengeful to the disobedient.

*[i teach them to hunt and fish in case renewed
times come i teach them to carve upon*

*the birch the stories of our ancient line
one of my daughters is near your age i worry
about her she knows the words to our people's*

*songs longs to sing in the day but her mother
and i stay her tongue we do not wish danger]*

Remember that strict submission
is the watchword of any Christian girl.
Stay mild and consider your masters' rules.

An Unworthy Servant of Christ,
Samson Occom

Boston, January 1767

When you own a child,
     can you treat her the same?
          I don't mean when you birth her,
     when you share a well of blood.—
This is a complicated space.
     There is slavery here.
          There is maternity here.
     There is a high and a low
that will last centuries.
     Every speck floating in this room
          must be considered.
     I don't want to simplify
what is breathing—
     choking—
          in this room, though there are those
     of you who will demand that I do.
Either way I choose, I'm going
     to lose somebody.
          I want to be human,
     to assume that because Susannah
had three offspring who died as children—
     the details gone
          about coughs that clattered
     on, rashes that scattered across
necks or chests,
     air that did not expel,
          never exhaled to cool tongues—
     that Susannah would be desperate
to cling to a new little girl.
     Her need to care, her fear,
          would rise into Psalms.
     When Phillis's face

was not her mirror,
        would that have mattered?
                When water did not drench
        Phillis's hair, but lifted it high
into kinks,
        would that have mattered?
                Can I transcribe the desire
        of a womb to fill again?
That a daughter was stolen
        from an African woman and given
                into a white woman's hands?
        And did Susannah promise the waft
of that grieving mother's spirit
        that she would keep this daughter safe
            yet *enslaved*—
and this
is the craggiest
hill I've ever climbed.

THE MISTRESS ATTEMPTS TO INSTRUCT
HER SLAVE IN THE WRITING OF A POEM

c. 1769

Note 1. This Verse to the End is the Work of another Hand.

— Addition by Phillis Wheatley at the bottom of "Niobe in Distress . . ."

phillis		*susannah*
these are my poems	*[no one else]*	saw you on that dock
writes my words	*[no one else]*	wanted to take you
since wood stopped	*[i remember]*	how thin you were
afric's fancy'd happy seat	*[don't remind me]*	i'm not your mother
of what i owe	*[to the Savior]*	i have prayed
who kept me	*[in dark abodes]*	you nearly died
from my despair	*[a benighted soul]*	knew nothing of God
He calls me *ethiop*	*[in the afterlife]*	those devils burn
negroes black as cain	*[may heavens rule]*	the chosen redeemed
may they lead you	*[to your mother]*	give your farewells
speak new greetings	*[in your hands]*	speak your prayers
though sorrows labor	*[on your quill]*	accept salvation
my mother calls	*[daughter]*	is that not enough

LOST LETTER #4: SAMSON OCCOM, MOHEGAN, TO SUSANNAH WHEATLEY, BOSTON

August 30, 1770

Dear Madam

I bring you longings of our Savior
who makes our lives possible upon
this invaded travail.

[my people scold me for believing wheelock's lies
that white man who promised to start a school

for the children of my kind he promised
rooms bordered by brick and wood
that he would teach them tricks of english

that man's a colorless devil like the one
who spoke scripture in the wilderness]

In prayer, Phillis's path came to me,
as she stands on my heart's sweet floor.
She is of an age to marry and sail back

to the clouds of her homeland, to bring
the Good News to the heathens.

[it is time for her to marry i have heard
talk from boston that many white men seek
to snatch a negress such as her this is

a dangerous moment she is too glorious
to stay alone i do not wish her destruction]

Why not let one of our African missionaries
take her hand, as God has ordained? —
If you could spare a coin, I would bless you.

Your Good for Nothing Servant,
Samson Occom

LOST LETTER #5: SUSANNAH WHEATLEY, BOSTON, TO SAMSON OCCOM, MOHEGAN

November 7, 1770

Dear Most Reverend Sir

I am glad your wife is clear of illness.
Family is most important, as well I know—
my dark child is dear and dutiful.

Please do not speak of her marriage,
but only affirm my better wisdom.

*[you crow so easily of my child going
to africa forever who would look after
her in that black pagan pit]*

I have judged that brambles of marriage
should not snag her—and who to marry?

*[do not dare talk of this to me again
you drunk painted creature no wonder wheelock
reneged on his promise to give you that school]*

What African man would be worthy of her?
What white man could she equal?

She is a child of no Nation but God's.
Minister,
our friendship means the earth to me:

I would be blessed if your prayers
told you to keep your own counsel.

*[you have not nursed that child heard her scream
and worse the nights of wishing for cries when
wheezing stole her before she returned*

*what man knows of this my husband was asleep
i shall not sacrifice i promised God to keep her safe]*

55

It gladdens me to know you have put strong
drink behind you and re-sown your faith.—
I send you a few coins, as is my Christian duty.

In Him,
Susannah Wheatley

January 30, 1771

Dear Miss Mary:

I know that marriage is a woman's
tithe, but this house is cold without you.
I know it is not my place to question

these patterns, why letters speak
a language, and then, the muses cry to me.

[i hope you find this letter in your reticule
i miss you already i thought to leave with you
until mistress held me back]

Yet if I could question Our Lord's Word,
I'd ask, why is marriage a woman's task?

[i have no sister of my own each time someone
leaves this house even for a short season i think
of that day i was cut from my earth]

Your mother has explained the stain
of Eve, but tells me, as a slave girl,

marriage is not for me, that I should be glad
that particular chain has passed me by—
I should focus on the Lord for my plight.

[what is it like to call a room your own to sit
in the middle and not on a corner stool

do you feel grand does the hand
weighted by your ring
make you free or mastered]

Your Phillis

How old was the child when she first laughed
in her master's kitchen? She shouldn't have
been eating at the table with the whites,

but Susannah might have flouted custom:
her woman's heart soft. Tender. Unboiled meat.
When the child was very small, Susannah

might have brought her into the dining room,
sat her on a stool, placed plain crockery
on the child's lap, engaged with her in English,

a caged music, but soon, that would end.
The child was enslaved: she'd need to learn of sin,
of Cain.—What was the time when she answered

to her new name? She would have stopped
saying those syllables in her own language,
My yaay didn't call me that. Enough

punishments—but hopefully, no whippings—
would have broken her boldness, the kissing
of teeth in imitation of her Nation.

When did she learn that white women
take care in this world, but black women
walk barefoot on glass? And what was the age

of Phillis when she stopped turning East,
thinking of water in faithful bowls,
of her parents,

of love only ending in death?
There is no such age. There never will be,
though a sister's mouth might tell you lies.

Book: Enlightenment

Misery is often the parent of the most affecting
touches in poetry.—Among the blacks is misery
enough, God knows, but no poetry . . . Religion
indeed has produced a Phyllis Whately, but
it could not produce a poet. The compositions
published under her name are below the dignity
of criticism.
— Thomas Jefferson, from *Notes on the State of Virginia*

The Negroes of Africa have by nature no feeling
that rises above the trifling . . .
— Immanuel Kant, from *Observations on
the Feeling of the Beautiful and the Sublime*

THE AFRICAN-GERMAN PHILOSOPHER ANTON WILHELM AMO RETURNS TO HIS HOME REGION IN WEST AFRICA TO BECOME A SAGE AND (POSSIBLY) A GOLDSMITH

Axim, Gold Coast, c. 1752

I am a well,
earth ravished: the more lust,
the deeper the color.
          A tangible thrust, which I craved
          back in Halle.
Why a woman touches
the bone at her neck,
a query of material and skin.
          I tried to explain this concept
          to my colleagues in their cold land,
along with the theory of crocodiles—
creatures which bare their teeth.
Philosophy did not pull them.
          What I am,
          what I am not.
Which one: the son
of an honorable family.
A man. A former slave.
          A body able to enter
          the maze of learning
and find and crush
the kernel negating
whole hosts.
          That's the riddle's end—
          or philosophy.

Now facts.
I wanted to come home.
I am here like this gold
            in my hand.
            It twists when heated.
It can choke.
It can adorn.
What it is,
            what it is not.

ILLUSTRATION: PETRUS CAMPER'S MEASUREMENT OF THE SKULL OF A NEGRO MALE

c. 1770

No, do not touch.
The instrument on that table
measures the dead.

I trust its use only to those sensitive

enough, who shall not crush
what once was flesh.
Here is a sturdy fellow—

take it.

There was wool on this skull.
Do not let this disconcert you:
Our Lord surely loves

all His upright children.

Remember that, though the measure
might tell you differently.
Look now at the forehead

where a vein was wont to bulge—

there the seams of good and evil met.
Even this Negro connected
to God's grace.

Place your thumb on that spot,

imagine the throbbing of the soul,
its climbing inside these fragile bars—
the absence thereof pains.

Sir, I promise you: sometimes—

yes, yes,
late at my labors—
I see the print of Eve's

thumb, the same she traced

down the spine of the adversary
before giving in.
O, she was a coy one!—

Notice here the flat nasal plane?

Despite one eye's close proximity
to the other, I have discovered
something through my observations:

my colleagues were mistaken.

This subject was not a brother
to the orangutan after all—
I know.

It was a jolt to me as well.

THE BEAUTIFUL AND THE SUBLIME

Immanuel Kant, Konigsberg, 1764

some ecstasies need
fulfillment   others merely exist
whip of branch

next to the tree's trunk
tease of light imprisoned
by shadow   my brilliance

next to another's duncery
our broken chain
against my newly found senses   to wit

first the keen whites
                    [i rise]
then the mean yellows
                    [i bathe and dress]
then the savage reds
                    [i break my fast]
then the trifling blacks
                    [i take my sweet walk]
the lowly apes at the last
                    [lonely contemplation]
first the keen whites
                    [i rise]

God i will know one day
or never   but the letter's
embrace   Reason's page crackling

the least of these gives
happiness   and no   i am
not such a stuffy man

PORTRAIT OF DIDO ELIZABETH BELLE LINDSAY, FREE MULATTO, AND HER WHITE COUSIN, THE LADY ELIZABETH MURRAY, GREAT-NIECES OF WILLIAM MURRAY, FIRST EARL OF MANSFIELD AND LORD CHIEF JUSTICE OF THE KING'S BENCH

c. 1779

Dido moves quickly—
as from the Latin *anime*.

Breath or soul.
Beside her, the generations-free kin,

a biscuit figurine in pink.
Dido positioned in irony—

the lowest are taller here.
Elizabeth should provide

an unkind contrast: pretty, blonde,
pale in uncovered places—

but no.
The painter worships the quickened Other.

Dido, his coquette of deep-dish
dimples, his careless, bright love.

Forget History.
She's a teenager.

We know what that means:
cocky, stupid about reality.

No thought of babies—
feathers in her arms.

She might wave them, clearing
dead mothers from the air—

and she's special—
her great-uncle dressed her with care,

hid her from triangles and seas
outside this walled garden.

Let her be.
Please.

No Dying Mythical
Queen weaving a vivid, troubled skin—

but Dido, full of girlhood,
and Elizabeth reaching

a hand. *Behave, cousin,*
she begs.

Don't run away from me.

Let justice be done, though the Heavens fall.
— *William Murray, Lord Chief Justice of the King's Bench*

I. Somerset v. Stewart, 1772

The defendant speaks:

As to the issue of baptism,
that drops of transmuted water
guarantee freedom, and one day
each soul may fly away
to Heaven, that is a contract
between my Negro and the good Lord.
God doesn't cost a thing—
no pound, no shilling—
but He doesn't make an African
free, either.
My ownership of my slave
is a contract of property
in England,
the West Indies,
and the American colonies.
My claim follows my slave
to the parted lips of the grave.
I want my veiny
property returned,
an acknowledgment
of what I own.

II. Gregson v. Gilbert, 1783

The plaintiff speaks:

As to the issue of murder,
that the captain of my slave ship
The Zong dumped nearly two
hundred pieces of valuable
black property into the sea,
I will admit his incompetence,
that his miscalculation
was unfortunate—
and very sad!
Had he time for *mercy*, he'd have cut
the Negroes' throats to spare them
the confrontation with the sharks.
My captain is a godly man.
He'd never have done this
to servants of Christ.
The safety of holy water would
have been a keen conundrum.
It is lucky the Africans
remained unbaptized, free
of the Lord's coverture—
as it is, I would sleep soundly,
were it not for the public
outcry of murder—
which is embarrassing to me—
and my need for the four
thousand pounds (or thereabouts)
of lost revenue, for which I am suing.
Those Africans are dead
and I am a businessman.

III. The Public Lord Mansfield v.
The Private William Murray, 1787

The defendant and plaintiff speak:

As to the issue of gossip,
that I give preferential treatment
to a Negress, dress her in colored
silks, bring her into the shadow
of British society—
Dido has become my child.
She was small when her father
brought her to me.
Unsteady, fat legs when she walked,
a tinge of gold murmuring
her mother's Nation, the hair
straight, spiked in wisps.
I cannot say whether my bride
and I would have reared her
had we known Dido's tone
would darken, her hair
rebel into wool—
but she's ours now.
When everyone else leaves
this old couple, Dido
has promised she will remain,
bringing us cups of sweet
milk from the cows
that she tends.
You let me protect
my kindred if you will cover
your own.
Natural law will stay:
morality and bones.

FOUND POEM: RACISM

Thomas Jefferson, 1787

The first difference which strikes
us is that of colour. Whether the black
     of the negro resides in the reticular
membrane between the skin
and scarf-skin, or in the scarf-skin
     itself; whether it proceeds from
the colour of the blood, the colour
of the bile, or from that of some
     other secretion, the difference
is fixed in nature, and is as real
as if its seat and cause were better
     known to us. And is this difference
of no importance? Is it not the foundation
of a greater or less share of beauty
     in the two races? Are not the fine
mixtures of red and white,
the expressions of every passion
     by greater or less suffusions of colour
in the one, preferable to that eternal
monotony, which reigns
     in the countenances,
that immoveable veil of black
which covers all the emotions
     of the other race?
Add to these, flowing hair, a more
elegant symmetry of form, their
     own judgment in favour of the whites,
declared by their preference of them,
as uniformly as is the preference
     of the Oranootan for the black

women over those of his own species.
The circumstance of superior beauty,
      is thought worthy attention
in the propagation of our horses,
dogs, and other domestic animals;
      why not in that of man?

Book: Awakening

'Twas mercy brought me from my Pagan land,
Taught my benighted soul to understand
That there's a God, that there's a Saviour too . . .
— Phillis Wheatley, from "On Being Brought
    from Africa to America"

Behold now, thy servant hath found grace in thy sight,
and thou hast magnified thy mercy, which thou hast
shewed unto me in saving my life . . .
— *Genesis* 19:19

. . . Should you, my lord, while you peruse my song,
Wonder from whence my love of Freedom sprung,
Whence flow these wishes for the common good,
By feeling hearts alone best understood,
I, young in life, by seeming cruel fate
Was snatch'd from Afric's fancy'd happy seat:
What pangs excruciating must molest,
What sorrows labour in my parent's breast? . . .
— Phillis Wheatley, from "To the Right Honourable
    William, Earl of Dartmouth"

STILL LIFE WITH GOD #1

Selina Hastings, Countess of Huntingdon, c. 1747

The core of *mercy*:
not intellect but
a nagging fire:
whether I am saved—
and how shall I know?
And is this belief
a blindness to my
moss-covered sin?
And when do I know
I shall leave distress
behind? My
husband died too soon
into our devotion—
he loved the Lord
as much as I—
and I try to imagine,
what my husband's
outstretched arms
will call in Heaven.
And is he really there?
And if all was decided
so long ago, when God
collected the spire
of my woman's rib
in His mouth, then
how are we to recognize
the chosen? And
what words will
we speak?

PHILLIS WHEATLEY IS BAPTIZED
AT OLD SOUTH CHURCH

Boston, August 18, 1771

My body needs fresh light   some calm   I
      want understanding of water's touch   I think
I know   He requires no more cost   It
      is *mercy* chasing me   I must

not flee   I remind myself that to be
      free means without and within and lonely
times though my life is softer than most and to
      keep airing my snatched hours would be

sinful   Still   Holy Ghost   At last   God
      but I must sit in the balcony   Nobody
in the sanctuary   A Negro   A New-England Christian loves
      a soul though not the skin   a lie for a

pious man but truth for the master
      We *sable* rest in secret places   No
body knows our troubles   our journeys   Despite
      Jordan's wide swath I swim to Him   The

King of Kings   Trickster spirit and bright
      hopeful moment   I come upon hosannas
The skies realign in revolution   a bright
      world   stolen like me   dear-Lords

of England   suddenly enemies and
      thunder claps illuminate the Word's bright
cries   I am dark and blessed.   Determined
      My mother and father   (unseen)   ask reverence

from their *Ethiop*   My kin   Sacraments of
      today   No water keeps glory away   My Sunday
hymn   No sin   Now   I shall open my eyes

LOST LETTER #7: PHILLIS WHEATLEY, BOSTON, TO OBOUR TANNER, NEWPORT

September 27, 1771

Dear Sister of My Nation:

I shiver at the other chance, that had your master
not been visiting those few days in summer,
had I not waited for my mistress to take her midday

rest, there would be no wonder: my new friend.
Had I not disobeyed her word, her concerns for

the flames in my chest—had I not stolen away,
there would be no you. Even my coughing
in the street was a benediction. How God anoints

us in the midst of madness! How happy I am
to be baptized and covered by His *mercy!*

*[dark coming over the water i was naked
but unaware of shame my mistress taught me
that God hates a bare body especially a black one]*

Your name a comfort, though how shall I spell you?
"Arbour," an astounding, shady grove that protects?

"Obour," the name of "stone" in your homeland?
Until I decide, I have turned to Apostle Paul: As slaves
and women, we speak the same words.

Once, there was distance that kept tongues hopeless.
Now, we are blood, no division between our waters.

*[you have my yaay's face i lie and say
i cannot remember her but sister
i do i do know my name]*

I pray, I am your long-time friend,
Phillis

LOST LETTER #8: OBOUR TANNER, NEWPORT, TO PHILLIS WHEATLEY, BOSTON

November 15, 1771

My Dearest Sister:

Spell me how you wish, for you have saved me.
Before your letter, no one gave a care for my name.
That day we met, I was walking to the pier

on my errand. On the right side of the city,
the water, and I was tired of brigs and schooners

bringing in the taken, our naked, shivering brethren.
Their eyes begging, and I, a slave and woman.
What could I do?

[taunting of the gulls that time on the water
i cannot forget the sailors their touching their grabbing]

Even thoughts of canoes from long ago trouble me.
The thickened rivers of my homeland,
the danger, no matter the sun's love. —

Your frantic chuffing on the cobblestones?
An odd gift.

I dropped my basket of dinner fish, uncaring
that my own mistress would scold. Your breath
calmed and we stood with no explanation.

I knew I loved you when you
did not speak of ships.

[i shall forget that time i pray my memories die
at least you understand the screaming the clenching
of my chest at night you understand]

Sister,
I am Obour or Arbour or Coromantee Woman

THOMAS WOOLDRIDGE DEMANDS THAT
PHILLIS WHEATLEY INSTANTLY COMPOSE
A POEM IN HONOR OF HIS FRIEND, WILLIAM,
THE RIGHT HONORABLE EARL OF DARTMOUTH

Boston, October 1772

If Missouri had existed for white men,
Woolridge would have been a *show me* white man.

In what would become Missouri there lived
Omaha, Illini, Ioway—no white men—

Niutachi, Osage, and some of the Quapaw.
British didn't own that: no stuff for white men,

but according to logic, Missouri was *savage*—
of course, God had made land for white men.

The visitor showed at King's Street, to John
Wheatley's house: nice residence for a white man.

He'd read Phillis's *supposed* poetry
but needed proof sufficient for a white man.

He told the *Negress*, write something on the spot,
passed her paper: the name of a white man—

she advised she was busy, so please return
that next day. (I'm thinking, *Mr. Rude White Man.*)

Was the *servant* angry? What she wrote
the visitor signified on rich, titled white men.

Phillis versed pain over slavery, her parents'
loss: they'd suffered because of white men.

Heroic rhymes, but not much meekness.
Umph, umph, umph: I guess she told that white man.

HOW PHILLIS WHEATLEY MIGHT HAVE OBTAINED THE APPROVAL OF EIGHTEEN PROMINENT WHITE MEN OF BOSTON TO PUBLISH HER BOOK OF POETRY

Boston, October 28, 1772

Did it even happen that way?
Her climbing the steps,
her body confronting

*[eighteen white men
one black girl]*

the group of them soldered
into combined authority?
Her master was there,

yet she was by herself—
the terror—
an examination of her mind

*[eighteen white men
one black girl]*

assembled to assess
a slave's capabilities,
to see if she even could read—

let alone write poetry.
And what of her humanity?
Think of her

*[eighteen white men
one black girl]*

as a Daniel in skirts,
armed with God's intentions.
A graceful prophet versus

the descendants of Puritans
and merchants. Would she
have spoken in careful tongues,

*[eighteen white men
one black girl]*

her personal Holy Ghost
filing down beasts' teeth?
Would she—

an innocent in the world—
have pushed power aside
or forced it to the knees?

*[eighteen white men
one black girl]*

That day, it's unclear.
She might have been at home,
while another meeting

on the other side of Boston
took place, but what
I do know is this:

*[eighteen white men
one black girl]*

even if there was no examination,
at some point, she smiled in white
men's faces to gain her freedom.

She smiled to stay alive.
She quickly wrote those elegies
for grieving white ladies—

*[eighteen white men
one black girl]*

I know, because
I've smiled. I've chewed on fear
and anger, I've tap-danced

to move ahead, because
I needed to survive like so
many Others did and do,

*[eighteen white men
one black girl]*

until we lie down for the last time
and rise up as our own black Gods.
Dear Reader,

laugh at my (non-white)
tears, at my self-pity.
You think I've imagined

*[eighteen white men
one black girl]*

this examination,
this balancing sham, but
Miss Phillis and I understand.

LOST LETTER #9: PHILLIS WHEATLEY, BOSTON, TO OBOUR TANNER, NEWPORT

October 28, 1772

Sister:

My mistress hovers kindly in the background,
and today, I was glad of her, that I could shun
the steps of the meetinghouse, though I wrote

the attestation myself. I stayed behind
as befitted my station and worried my sewing.

[would they have looked at my teeth my ankle
brushing against the inside of my petticoats
believed i'm not an animal that i'm God's child]

There were days of waiting, before Master
Nathaniel returned the paper to me, the signatures

of those men overtaking the page.
[my narrow servant's smile would have been
no match for ledgers and pounds and shillings

men men men clustered prodding my quill my word
the things they did in the name of God the things]

I thank Providence for meetinghouses.—
For now, I write my elegies, of which I enclose one
for the sister of our Nation whose child was lost.

Please read my words to her—if she requires—
say I have journeyed and keep more than I speak.

Your Phillis

c. December 1, 1772

Phillis settles on a stool in the corner.
Separate and not equal, but maybe,
she doesn't squat on the floor
as the white women drink their tea.
There probably isn't a cup for her.
Though a poet, she's still enslaved,
but I'm betting Susannah will wrap
some food, save it in cloth
for later. Carefully, otherwise, bread
will become crumbs. The ladies
begin with an inventory of the dead:
husbands, siblings, babies—
this will be a touchy, morbid subject
for you, Dear Reader, as you live
in a time of trained doctors, medicines
tested before they are dispensed, eclectic
contraptions that resurrect the ailing—
but this is a time when Death dressed
in satin clothes, fine-knit hose
covering his knees. His cobbler had crafted
him noiseless shoes to sneak into
an infant's room and seal a mouth.
The grave was a constant each time
Phillis dressed in her modest garb—
a Puritan's stepdaughter
in drab dress, *de rigueur* bonnet,
woolen cloak hiding her girl-shoulders—

and visited Susannah's coterie
of reading Boston ladies. Phillis prayed
she wouldn't have to write another elegy
to sooth a white lady's grief. Each time,
her lost mother wails in her,
as she composes a poem that never salves.
Next week: a new batch of elegies.

Muses: Convening

. . . even when she, in a sacred grove, with each hand
in that of a tender Parent, was paying her devotions
to the great Orisa who made all things . . .
— Belinda Sutton, from "Petition to the Massachusetts
    General Court"

When [Ona Judge was] asked if she is not sorry
she left Washington, as she has labored so much
harder since, than before, her reply is, "No, I am
free, and have, I trust been made a child of God
by the means."
— from "Interview with Ona Maria Judge," 1845

i say the stones marked an old tongue and it was called
eternity . . .
— Lucille Clifton, from "mulberry fields"

BLUES: YEMOJA

                         Here are the children   Mama
         those I will gather   Mami
                                        those I will lose
                  Yemoja & I am blues
                                                & suffering
                        diving in & clutching
         what is subcutaneous
                                        & deeper chord
         I am snapping my spear
                                                at pale stepsisters
                        nymphs swatting tails
                                        hitting the waves
         calling to their fathers
                        One man with trident
                                        entrailing a swimming whale
         Another man speaking
                                        tongues of vain apostles
         who cast their nets
                        & I am trying
                        to save my children
         from a third man
                                        & his follies
                        a seaman teaching
                                loud legacies
                  washing his beard in salt
         & I
                        Yemoja
                  combing sinful shores
                                        chanting proverbs
                        hoping to retrieve
         my children from water
                                recalling when people lived
                                their days at will

so many bones had risen

                                          seed awoken

        open eyes

                & soon enough

trouble

          & I am she

                    Mami who rocks her children

in water

        Mama who pulls the caul

              tight in water

Yemoja gathers

            prophet water

                    ship's water

        every living

              creeping thing water

& I am she

            speaking of old ones wrapped

                in cowries of promise

      how they flapped

              their blue gums in prayer

how they clung

                to the firmament

        as traders descended

                    with chains

           My children   *oh*

I need to save them   *oh*

            These are my blues   *oh*

my words

         my solid sand

the bottom of distressed seas

                The drowned ones become

        sculptures of memory   *oh*

        Who called this time   *oh*

Who had this vision
     Who named these days
the air broken with shame
       these many-throated birds
these ephemeral babels
     carrying forth shrouds
of praisesong
    So many waves
         ocean sea
     river tears
all the years
    all the slaves
    & all the chains
        that know me
children born to griot verses
      talk drums over distance
   let the harbingers
         of bent rivers
      & dammed twigs
call out from their graves
     Mama *oh*
    Mami *oh*
my sweet water
     my good water
   how many names
& I
      Yemoja
   black and remembering

amnesiac wood

nostrils of girls	who was bought	uncle's hand
guts on the air	who was sold	defeated man
history's charnel	i say	trader's silver

sailing knot to knot

naked in the corner	door of no return	sing the mutiny
in the slave house	sniff bougainvillea	who is ashamed
i say	ready dawn's kill	naked in the corner

jealous sharks

i shall	who did	i say
they did	i'm here	my name
who shall	i say	yes here

on the battlefield

call woman	call america	call revolution
call the brother	call the myth	i say
call the auction	call africa	call the sachem

in God's name

is this called	is my mother	is some kin
i say	is this called	is some water
is my mother	i say	is this called

ISABELL

Virginia Colony, c. 1621

Like any love should be,
hers was touch and never leave.
Some arguments and tears with Antoney,
her husband, but no freedom.
They were tied, a curt blessing
in that era of dark skin and kin.
Separations would occur soon enough,
but they had to band together,
this woman and her man who might
have come on a ship with eighteen others.
Isabell cooked for him from flesh
he trapped or caught.
They might have looked at the entrails
of his prey to decipher
what the day had been,
back home in Africa.
What would the drums say?
Was it a feast time?
Was their village in the same spot?
When their son was born, Isabell
probably kept him away
from others for several days.
That night, when the necessary
seclusion was done, Antoney
would have shaved the baby's
head and spat in his ear.
Tapped a foot on the floor,
told an unforgotten story.
And then, Isabell put the baby
to her breast and sang,
Your name is William here,
but Mother calls you
something else,
something old in secret.

DEFINITIONS OF HAGAR BLACKMORE

Middlesex County, Massachusetts, April 1669

I. BLACKAMOOR
a. Negar, nigger, jigaboo.
Inversion. *Blacker than me.*
b. A word describing many tribes.
c. After the anchoring, a name separating
light and dark, literate and unlettered,
house and field.

II. HAGAR
a. A female slave who flies away,
as the Greek indicates.
b. Someone meant to have less than,
whose children are meant
to have less, as well.
c. The handmaid of Sarai, later Sarah.
A slave who was given
to Abram to rape, since she did
not give her permission to be given.
d. A woman who smirks at her pale
sister: *If I'm not free, you can't be either.*

III. HAGAR BLACKMORE
a. A Negress of the seventeenth century.
b. A woman stolen from Angola,
who cannot escape category.
c. A resident of an empired land.
d. A resister whose spine
will not touch sheet.
e. A curser of men
blocking the sight
of God's well.

THE REPLEVIN OF ELIZABETH FREEMAN
(ALSO KNOWN AS MUM BETT)

Great Barrington, Massachusetts, May 1781

I was hit by my mistress
or I was not.
I stood between her
and my black child
or I did not.
And who must speak for me
in order for you to believe? —
If a white man says a word,
that word is true, can squat
upon a mountain, and behold,
it will spread its gospel.
But if a Negro crows a vowel,
it halts upon the ground
until a white man says *rise*.
Why is it that you can lie
all by yourself and walk away,
but my truth is dismissed,
though I bring
a thousand witnesses? —
A white man had to plead
my case in court,
in order for me to be free,
and so, at the end of my life
what I shall hold onto
is a gold necklace
and a gravestone
inscribed with the title
of *efficient helper*.
Perhaps some kindness
because I tended to white
children's seeking mouths
before my own child
could eat.

THE JOURNEY OF ONA JUDGE, ENSLAVED SERVANT OF MARTHA WASHINGTON, WIFE OF PRESIDENT GEORGE WASHINGTON

I. From Virginia to New York (1789)

That spring mistress took me from green-spoked lands
and my poor mother stayed behind to tend
her fears: her dear girl quivered from her hands.

Packed in a coach to New York, lonely band
of powerless slaves, forced to move, to bend
for Master, to leave our Virginia lands.

No choices, no kind of voice, what demands
could we make? We said, *Yes sir*, then we went
on the journey after clutching the hands

of our beloveds. *So long green-spoked lands—*
and songs and family and peace and friends.
I kissed my mother, then dropped from her hands.

But up north, freedmen approached, whispered grand,
pure, clouds: my mistress couldn't keep me penned.
Those words, a paradise released, green land

that hinted of trees, a river, a banned
song: *Here, you are free. Your bondage must end.*—
Then, Master took me to Virginia lands.
My chance for freedom laughing in my hands.

II. Virginia to Philadelphia (1789–1796)

A devil's trick, a fear of letting go,
a lowdown word took me to southern lands,
then back north again, else the law would throw

me in freedom's light: my mistress's foe.
She gave me wages, hugs, offered her bland
smiles meant to keep me. She would not let me go.

She praised my hard work, regaled freedom's woes,
told me which Negroes I could not hold hands
with, talk to, smile at, or else they would throw

my virtue in harsh light, find fields and sow
sin with this girl, make despicable plans
of male trickery to make me let go

of my sweet life with my owners in tow.
One night, I heard her, while I was rambling
in the hallway: she revealed that she'd throw

me to her kin, a gift. It was a blow
to me, a loyal girl, a steady hand
for Mistress when grief would not let her go:
at dinner time, I walked out the front door.

III. The Land of Relative Contentment (1845)

I'm a small woman, no need to be grand.
Those folks dogged me, but Death made them let go.
I'm a firebrand: I took my freedom's throw.

FOR THE FIRST OF SEVERAL TIMES, BELINDA SUTTON, FORMER ENSLAVED SERVANT OF THE HOUSE OF ISAAC ROYALL, PETITIONS THE MASSACHUSETTS GENERAL COURT FOR A PENSION IN HER OLD AGE

February 14, 1783

i shall trust the new word
of this country
freedom

                        i shall not call the names
                        of the dead

in that taken
child's place
here is *Belinda*

                        toiling in unnatural cold
                        i ask for bits of what you sing

what you hold so dear
i say   i have a woman's
memory

                        men of war
                        fingering silver or cowrie

those men had no thought
for me
only the blue in front

                        cruel schemes
                        stricken drums

i say
i ask for less than what is written
in some Book or on

                    the gathered conscience
                    i know you have

more than that
too much
understanding in this life

                    remains a brick mansion
                    pennies in exchange

for what was taken from me
i say   i ask in my free
Gods' names

                    the Orisha
                    always

they are here when
i look around at this
newfound place

                    and i say   Oshun
                    Obatala

i say
Shango
Yemoja

                    and i say   Oya
                    Esu-Elegbara

like you they sail
and anchor where
they please

                    and yes
                    they too crave

Book: Voyage

I was receiv'd in England with such kindness,
Complaisance, and so many marks of esteem
and real Friendship as astonishes me on the
reflection, for I was no more than 6 weeks there . . .
— Phillis Wheatley, from a letter to David Wooster,
    October 18, 1773

Adieu, New-England's smiling meads,
    Adieu, the flow'ry plain:
I leave thine op'ning charms, O spring,
    And tempt the roaring main . . .
— Phillis Wheatley, from "A Farewel to America"

PHILLIS WHEATLEY EMBARKS FROM BOSTON ON HER SEA VOYAGE TO LONDON

May 8, 1773
. . . [In London] was presented with a Folio Edition of Milton's
Paradise Lost, printed on a Silver Type, so call'd from its
Elegance, (I suppose) . . .
—Letter from Phillis Wheatley to David Wooster, October 18, 1773

Milton was infamous (and dead)
when they placed Phillis in that first boat.

He'd contemplated the scales of evil:
soft skin of a woman,

patriarch wronged by love—
several lifetimes of suffering iambs.

The poets' common woes would come much later.
Darkness: God's gift, Satan's hiss.

The blind master and his precocious
apprentice divided by color, Reason,

and a hundred-some years.
When Phillis crossed that sea again,

a teenager, she might have closed her eyes,
hoped to stroke the triangle's rim.

Milton wouldn't reconcile himself to blindness,
to cringing to upright men.

No one would sell Phillis away from her parents
because Ham wasn't damned in the Bible.

She would go back twelve years
to a childhood in a lost Gambia.

The clock would break.
The Muses wouldn't love her.

They'd strip her of the letters
of the English alphabet.

She'd be a stranger to Christ—
to fame, to Homer's antique name,

to the eyes of the prying, master race.

LOST LETTER #10: MARY WHEATLEY LATHROP, BOSTON, TO PHILLIS WHEATLEY, LONDON

May 9, 1773

Dear Phillis

Mama is sick and failing. She forbade me
to run to the harbor and call you back, but as
soon as your ship sailed, I began to write this.

*[when will this reach you oh please come
home she is dying i believe oh please]*

I know if your hands were laid on Mama's
skin, she would stop hugging the bed.
She is so proud of you, little one!

*[papa is frightened and angry at everybody
he does not speak his fears]*

I have done my best to bid her to rise. —
And how is our brother Nathaniel?
Has his countenance been cleared?

*[you take the place of mama's dead babies
as for me no children though my husband*

*reads to me about sarai's womb filled late in life
mama is afraid for you over there one night
when fever rose from her chest she cried*

*that nathaniel might sell you to some man
she saw your neck fastened by silver]*

I hope your times in London are joyful
and that your words find devotees.
Do what God tells you in prayer.

Affectionately,
Mary

PHILLIS WHEATLEY WALKS BESIDE HER MASTER'S SON, NATHANIEL, ON THE STREETS OF LONDON

June 1773

His rib was a tether, but she noticed
there were other Africans in the city
of London: the slaves of the rich,
their necks encased in silver.
Others were free, but in rags, bespoke
tales of poverty, their collarbones
begging for another metal:
the heavy, soft gold of their African homelands.
Maybe Phillis passed by a marketplace,
with other Negroes shouting their wares—
and she revisited her memories of walking
with her mother in the hot Gambia.
The baskets of peanuts, gaudy perfume
of mangos in a row. Plantains, hibiscus,
printed cloth with arcs of red, yellow,
black, green. Bright consolations,
as when somebody tracks her heart
into the road of another.
In the mother's earlobes, bride gifts dangling—
the little girl wore a matching nose ring,
the pride she'd refuse to part with,
until her death. And that untaken
child could run from Yaay's side,
but always return to familiar
road and known dust.

In the second yard are: I. Rover and Phillis,
two ravenous wolves from Saxony.
— A Companion to Every Place of Curiosity and Entertainment
in And About London and Westminster . . .

To get to that place of curiosity
in the Tower, to the second yard where you see
a wolf who bears your second name,
you must become a spectacle
    in turn. Be pleasant. Pretend you aren't
insulted when you hear, "How's it feel, Miss Phillis,
now that you're no longer a barbarian?"
Learn to ease from white men who
    might want tastes of dark meat,
to nibble on your brilliance, you who
are shoring up what you have inside,
reminding yourself of luck: You could be
    in a cage at the bottom of a slave
castle, passed around from white man
to white man, instead of in London,
celebrated in parlor after parlor.
    At least, you aren't naked.
At least, you aren't being raped.
At least, they only give you presents and money.
You must meet Lord Dartmouth,
    Alderman Kirkman, Lord Lincoln,
the famous Dr. Solander, Israel Moduit,
Brooks Watson, Benjamin Franklin,
Baron George Lyttelton, John Thornton—
    and Granville Sharp, the white
abolitionist who tells you how he helped
to free Brother Somerset, and Mr. Sharp
takes you to the Tower of London to see
    the animal who is called by your name.

There, the whips hit stone.
There, the cries of *behave*.
There, the outrage of the wolf that wishes
        to be freed, or at least eat in peace
without being watched.
To see your creature namesake,
you must travel from Boston to London.
                Travel from The Gambia to Boston.
Travel from your parents'
arms to a cage filled with other
enslaved people who may
        or may not speak your language.
You must quiet your eventual anger.
that men the same color as you
took currency in exchange for selling
        you away from your parents.
that soon, because of your color,
slave-trading white men will consider
you kin to slave-trading black men
        who didn't
and don't consider you any
dearer than a wolf.
You must wade through shackled people,
        a tight, metaphysical web.
Hands reaching to you,
a little girl, begging for salvation.
You must face the plank of the ship
        the door of no return, the graveyard-sea,
call on the *mercy* of your Maker.
You must—
you must.
        You have to sail.

ILLUSTRATION: A MUNGO MACARONI /
A BLACK ENGLISHMAN OF SARTORIAL SPLENDOR

c. 1772

As splashing as I am
in these close
breeches you
might expect
naughtiness, that I kiss
the dented bottom
lips of moneyed
white ladies
or pretty gentlemen,
after bowing
and sweeping
off this hat.
I shall (or shan't)
give in to pleasure.
Look down at my shoes.
The leather distressed
so well, soft
as Christ's sympathy.
I confess,
I am vainglorious.
I snatch after life
as I please, bespoke
or nothing else—
thrills loosed
from silver collars.

July 10, 1773

Dear Sister

Hello from London! I am ablaze
with happiness, but Master Nathaniel

must stay unimpressed: when we walked
the singing streets—"Too many people"—
when we toured the Queen's House—

"Why so much space for one woman?"
He gripped my hand, leaving red stripes,

saying, Mistress "would kill" him when
we returned to Boston, if he lost "her best child."
Here are prettily dressed Negroes, and talk

of Brother Somerset who won freedom in court.
Yet others wear silver collars, shiny misery.

John Thornton (friend of my mistress),
has cautioned humility, that God has anointed
me—a Negro and woman—with special gifts.

*[the water sailing here wide i need no choking
silver i'm a woman tied to whatever man cares for me]*

I met Benjamin Franklin, of kite
and lightning fame—Master Nathaniel muttered,
"Go to the old debaucher"—and stayed in

his room, but Franklin only needed
me to recite quotes from Pope's Homer.

[that old man asked could i remember my
journey away from my first home his face ashine
with pink eagerness satan dressed in ease]

Then, I slid into the Book of Jonah, a poor
man cast like me from a creature's belly.

[my chest ratcheted with fire the nightmares
of dying i cannot remain here free my mistress
is sick she snatches my arm from across the water]

In the morning, we return to a shop
where Master Nathaniel encountered a pretty

young lady that he insists on searching for.
These things I do in the service
of someone else's love.

Yours,
Phillis

LOST LETTER #12: PHILLIS WHEATLEY, LONDON, TO SUSANNAH WHEATLEY, BOSTON

July 15, 1773

Dear Mistress:

I have decided to sail back to you. I am safe
here, but there is no home. Your hearth
is nowhere in this place, your call lost throughout

a room. I've not forgotten you, please no fear,
and my tears shall flow until I see you again.

I hear my voice in this city but only when I shout.
I come out onto the street, look for the narrow
measures of Boston, but here things are wide.

[i love you but how long shall you keep me captive
i traveled to leave your hold to suck air into a mouth

i own i could slide away from the rib of nathaniel
here are brethren waiting to help me i could let go
of his coat i could run through this crowd but then

i should be a woman alone and if you died while
i am here i wonder if God would keep me]

My Lady, the Countess of Huntingdon,
has been too busy to greet me. I am grieving,
as I'd prayed she'd find a moment to receive.

[and then i would have bowed and curtseyed
and played my teeth to that nosy old white woman]

My mistress, I have been a good girl—
I shall stay that way and sail to your hands
soon. Please hold on.

Your servant and child,
Phillis

July 25, 1773

Dear Mother:

Your favorite child is healthy, and as for
your scarcely cherished son, I am flourishing.
For a servant, Phillis has had adventures.

[everyone knows that girl takes the place
of your dead children don't try to decline that truth

i know you lean towards freeing her but I am
of another mind what money we would till from
her what white men would pay to hear and touch]

Benjamin Franklin paid us a visit, we stayed
a week with your friend John Thornton,

and I am afraid Phillis grows too large
with the slathered praise of white men.
You should speak to her of moral weakness

when she arrives back in Boston. —
I shall stay in England a longer while.

By the time I return home, I expect
that you will have rebuked your bed.
I send Phillis home in the care of Captain Calef.

[how like a fool i look escorting a blackamoor
without a collar as if she were my Negro wife

let us see how phillis fares on that ship alone
as a negress if her virtue survives the journey
i pray for her to be ruined and chastened]

Your son,
Nathaniel

FOUND POEM: PROOF

Front Matter from Phillis Wheatley's Book of Poetry, 1773

To the PUBLICK.

AS it has been repeatedly suggested
to the Publisher, by Persons, who have seen
      the Manuscript, that Numbers would be ready
to suspect they were not really the Writings
      of PHILLIS, he has procured the following
Attestation, from the most respectable
      Characters in *Boston*, that none might have
the least Ground for disputing their *Original.*
      WE whose Names are under-written, do assure
the World, that the POEMS specified in the following
      Pages, were (as we verily believe) written by PHILLIS,
a young Negro girl, who was but a few Years
      since, brought an uncultivated Barbarian
from *Africa*, and has ever since been,
      and now is, under the Disadvantage
of serving as a Slave in a Family in this Town.
      She has been examined by some of the best
Judges, and is thought qualified to write them.
      His Excellency THOMAS HUTCHINSON,
Governor, The Hon. ANDREW OLIVER,
      Lieutenant-Governor.
The Hon. Thomas Hubbard,
      The Rev. Charles Chauncey, *D.D.*
The Hon. John Erving,
      The Rev. Mather Byles, *D.D.*
The Hon. James Pitts,
      The Rev. Ed. Pemberton, *D.D.*
The Hon. Harrison Gray,
      The Rev. Andrew Elliot, *D.D.*
The Hon. James Bowdoin,
      The Rev. Samuel Cooper, *D.D.*

John Hancock, *Esq*;
    The Rev. Mr. Samuel Mather, *D.D.*
Joseph Green, *Esq*;
    The Rev. Mr. John Moorhead, *D.D.*
Richard Carey, *Esq*;
    Mr. John Wheatley,
her Master.

Book: Love

Since my return to America my Master, has at the desire
of my friends in England given me my freedom. The Instrument
is drawn, so as to secure me and my property from the hands
of the Executrs. adminstrators, &c. of my master, & secure
whatsoever should be given me as my Own . . .
— Letter from Phillis Wheatley to David Wooster,
    October 18, 1773

Love me, honey, love me true?
Love me well ez I love you?
An' she answe'd, "'Cose I do" . . .
— Paul Lawrence Dunbar, from "A Negro Love Song"

LOST LETTER #14: JOHN PETERS, BOSTON, TO PHILLIS WHEATLEY, BOSTON

January 21, 1774

My Dearest Miss Wheatley,

Please excuse my temerity in handing this
letter to Sister [—] and asking her to plead
my case: I pray I have not acted in haste.

*[i love the ring in your nose my mother said
in our homeland the dame adorns a precious child]*

I have waited for a ripe time, though I am
infected with caution, for what should I say
to the Greatest Poetess of our Nation?

That you hold Beauty in tight clasp there
is no question, but I am in awe of your poesy.

*[across the water i would visit your father
and ask for your bride price he would say there
is no amount too high for a woman such as you]*

May I be allowed to say that on Sabbath, I have
observed you from our perch in the balcony,

your joy at the Savior's words? Miss Wheatley,
will you take my favor to heart? If you will not
cherish me, at least, will you not discard?

*[they say you were feted in england you may travel
there again woman please don't leave here is a black*

*man in front of you i am not afraid to love you
in the old african ways here is someone your father
would accept woman i am asking for your hand]*

From your most devoted admirer,
Master John Peters, Esquire

January 29, 1774

Dear Master Peters:

I received your favor, and I give thanks
to God that one of my Nation should
speak so highly of my low gifts.

[and who are you negro you are too pretty
your teeth too white your shoulders too high

i have seen you looking but can you even read
or did someone else scrawl out that letter
how dare you presume my baay was a man

like no other who rose to whisper in light he
knew what labor was though he never wore a pair

of shoes but you with that yellow kerchief
around your neck when you pass me i see
nothing in your hands they say you labor only

through speech sell groceries practice law doctor
placing leeches on the body to fill with kin]

I am but a basin through which
the desires of our Savior calls,
a clarion of paper and word.

In Christ,
Miss Phillis Wheatley

LOST LETTER #16: SUSANNAH WHEATLEY, BOSTON, TO PHILLIS WHEATLEY, BOSTON

March 3, 1774

My Girl,

The work of woman is to withstand,
to comprehend death is at hand always.

[john born 21 december 1746]

I urge you never to marry or bear
children, never to task the breakable

body that has been chastised
since eviction from the Garden.

Most times, your baby dies, and no elegy
shall calm that howl: I am weak.

[susannah born 15 may 1748]

I know pain that you cannot conceive.
When your third child stops breathing as well—

the softness so real upon a full breast—
for Mother there is no rest, no sleep.

*[here lyes sarah who died 11 may 1752
aged 7 yrs 9 months and 18 days]*

I am leaving, but please remember to keep
Christ at the helm of this earthly ship.

Your mother and mistress,
Susannah

May 1, 1774

Dear Miss Phillis

Your word reached me concerning
your mistress passing. She was the tallest
tree of modesty, charity and virtue.

Yet she would not rest on her laureled bed
if she knew you had walked away

from the duty of a married woman.
There are two men of your nation,
Bristol Yamma and John Quamine.

Both wrote your departed mistress's friend,
John Thornton, to press their suits.

What a sanctified journey you might
take with either of these Africans,
to minister to the heathens of your homeland!

*[i am afraid for you should nathaniel return
child it doesn't matter if you're free think on*

*the scheming he could sing he could sell you
look how he has ruined his father's legacy
would he not do the same to your flesh]*

Your gift of verse is not yours, but Heaven's.
Allow me to remind you of Ephesians,

that you must submit to a man's bridle—
an unanchored woman is not clean. God
does not want you cast in renewed darkness.

[for the sake of your soul the Lord's favor
and your safety you need to marry and you
a sickly girl requiring a man's tending hand]

Your good for nothing servant in Christ,
Samson Occom

August 1, 1774

My dear Phillis

I bring you greetings of our Savior,
Who will provide a balm for your recent
grief, the loss of your dear, guiding mistress.

I will be direct: I believe you need to marry.
This is a common feeling, for I've heard from

our friend, Reverend Occom. Like me, he
hopes you would sail to your homeland,
bringing the Good News to the heathens.

These two Africans who wish to take your hand—
Bristol Yamma or John Quamine—

What of them? Both are good suitors:
either would make a strong, Christian husband—
they'd direct your needy feet.

*[it is time for you to marry i have heard talk
from boston that foul black men seek a woman*

*such as you child you are a negress and given
to low appetites no matter your knowledge
of latin i do not want your destruction]*

I pray you are faring well. Whispers
of war give uncertain times for us,
the Lord's faithful children.

Your elder in Christ,
John Thornton

FREE NEGRO COURTSHIP #1

....

Phillis Wheatley and John Peters, Boston, c. Fall 1774

I like to dream
that Phillis and John stepped
in a time that didn't pay mind
to the sounds of Boston.
In the sanctuary of these
two throats: talking drums.
That his fingers were impatient,
cracking and aching
to touch the kinks beneath her cap.
But the brother was smarter than that.
He knew to take his time—
permission lay a long way off.
In these thin days before war,
he wished in vain for gold to give her,
the bride price to press his suit,
as he might have across the water.
Perhaps John sought out a sister
at church to give his first letter to,
and then, another brother in town
who acted as chaperone,
who gave John a sign that Phillis
was allowing him to court her.
I like to dream he was a cane-sweet
man who could not break apart,
that John had pretty white teeth.

FRAGMENT #1: FIRST DRAFT OF AN EXTANT LETTER, PHILLIS WHEATLEY, BOSTON, TO JOHN THORNTON, LONDON

October 30, 1774

Dear Sir

. . . You propose my returning to Africa
with Bristol yamma and John Quamine
~~who on earth are these negroes and how could~~
~~you hand me off as if this was once again an auction~~
if either of the upon Strict enquiry is Such,
as I dare give my heart and hand to, ~~as my body~~
~~is my own as my head is my own as my desire~~
~~is my own~~ I believe they are either of them
good enough if not too good for me,
or they would not be fit for missionaries;
~~though even the Lord has made cockroaches~~
~~and rats for whatever purpose He sees fit~~
but why do you hon'd Sir, wish those poor
men so much trouble as to carry me
So long a voyage? Upon my arrival, how like
a Barbarian Should I look to the Natives;
~~how like a brand-new captive how like a brand-new~~
~~slave a brand-new apple on eden's tree~~
I can promise that my tongue shall be quiet
for a strong reason indeed being an utter
stranger to the Language of Anamaboe.
Now to be Serious, This undertaking
Appears too hazardous, and not sufficiently
Eligible, to go—and leave my British
& American Friends—I am also unacquainted
with those Missionaries in Person. ~~and as~~
~~of today i have a good man i have a love~~
~~a hope and world of my own~~ . . .

FREE NEGRO COURTSHIP #2

Phillis Wheatley and John Peters, Boston, c. Winter 1775

Black John's slowing down,
      his feet on cobblestones.
            Waiting, listening for nosy gawkers—
no, there was safety—his sneaking
to the side alley off Queen Street.
      And there she was: his black Phillis.—
            I'm unafraid of watered memories,
      but this is a poem in which tragedy
can't be invoked, as when a black mama
      reminds you, "You know God don't like ugly."—
            The first time, a careful kiss
      between two sets of black lips.
Breathing together.
      The next time, when
            black separation grew unthinkable.
      Days and weeks and months,
until John spoke his wish:
      after the death of Susannah,
            the Wheatleys' house was no longer
      home for Phillis. Maybe,
if he did things right,
      she might link her black life with his.
            His desire to protect her from ships,
      step between his black woman and sailors.
His vow that sang over water
      to where her black parents might hear:
            He didn't just desire their black daughter—
he was honorable. He *intended*.—

It's not hard for me to conjure this,
        to have no black shame in their black joy.
           These black people,
       these *Free Negroes*, are my own,
and they had love.
        They still do:
           I'm still here.

LOST LETTER #19: PHILLIS WHEATLEY, PROVIDENCE, TO JOHN PETERS, BOSTON

January 25, 1776

Dear Master Peters:

[beloved i hope you are not too saucy
in the face of the redcoats please remember
that if they mistreat a white colonist

they will kill a negro please take care
i cannot bear to be this distance from you

my chest aches and not from sickness
i hope my kisses and letters have given
you oaths you never have to worry of another

african and as for white men i could not bear
their touch your skin glows with boldness

your beauty is home to me i did not want
to leave boston to leave you but when
the redcoats came miss mary made me

i owe her so much her mother so much
and now miss mary watches me she does

not wish me to leave her house to let
a negro drink from my gourd she is
not my family but when susannah died

i had no one else please do not scold me
if you are waiting for me all will be well
my love my love my love my love my love]

I pray you are safe and thriving in Boston,
and I remain your fellow servant in Christ,

Miss Phillis Wheatley

LOST LETTER #20: FROM JOHN PETERS, BOSTON, TO PHILLIS WHEATLEY, PROVIDENCE

March 18, 1776

My Love:

The streets are finally empty of redcoats,
the cobblestones relieved. Had I
not been free, I would have left Boston

when the soldiers departed, instead
of waiting for your return from Providence.

*[oh woman i cannot be angry with you it is only
that my bed is calling my love i need to marry
you to kiss that mouth filled with the muses]*

So many of our brethren skipped behind
the British, but where are they now?

*[i do not trust the word of any white man
you will not see me boarding any ship
my friend was tricked that way*

*i have not heard from him since he tapped up
that plank they say he toils a slave in jamaica]*

I would not leave you for any promise.
You own me now, the knotted
bone that jails my heart and future.

*[woman please come be with me as soon
as we may take our vows there is nothing*

*to keep you in a white man's house
you owe your masters curses why speak
of guilt why grant them credit for freedom]*

Your John

Catalog: Revolution

. . . in every human Breast, God has implanted
a Principle, which we call Love of Freedom; it is
impatient of Oppression, and pants for Deliverance . . .
— Letter from Phillis Wheatley to Samson Occom,
    February 11, 1774

Mrs Phillis, Your favour of the 26th of October
did not reach my hands 'till the middle of December.
Time enough, you will say, to have given an answer
ere this. Granted. But a variety of important occurrences,
continually interposing to distract the mind and withdraw
the attention, I hope will apologize for the delay, and plead
my excuse for the seeming, but not real, neglect.
— Letter from General George Washington to Phillis Wheatley,
    February 26, 1776

(ORIGINAL) BLACK LIVES MATTER: IRONY

Boston c. 1765

Scattered kin, men auctioned by British sires—
    bully tendrils of power, reaching down

for centuries: they arrived to acquire
    Native lands and spill that blood for the crown.

British stalking the foreign streets, choke, rough
    up those who misbehave, who dare to meet

soldiers' eyes, decry monarchy: *Resist.*
    The Americans fight back, begin to greet

Redcoats with sneers, in tracts call themselves *slaves.*
    Insist they're tethered, yet the Africans—

the many souls, the wretched, the taken
    who move from *human* to *trafficked*—

are ignored as white men don paper chains,
    the language of wounded throats, chatteled claims.

BLUES: HARPSICHORD, OR, BOSTON MASSACRE

The Death of Crispus Attucks, March 5, 1770

The language of wounded throats, chatteled wings.
    This for black men, but for their masters? Toys.

Music of the rich, a myth in near-spring,
    tame, wet times of careful, bewigged white boys

whose wives pretend blindness, play weak games, sway
    in tight panniers, their waists bone-threaded.

(Taken care of.) In this calm scene, there's lace—
    outside—reality—slippery steps

to walk, and then: stinking wharfs, those big ships
    disgorging tea and African stuffing.

Redcoats shoot Crispus-the-brave on streets slick
    with outrage and brethren's gore, snow muffling

truth, deaf to the harpsichord's free, blued daze.
    Black prelude. Black fugue. Black glittered affray.

FELIX (OF UNKNOWN LAST NAME) WRITES THE FIRST OF SEVERAL PETITIONS THAT WILL BE OFFERED BY AFRICANS TO THE MASSACHUSETTS GENERAL COURT, ASKING FOR THE FREEDOM OF ALL SLAVES

January 6, 1773

Prelude: comes a glittered affray that we
    paper with prayer, demand that you grant

Scripture's verity: admit we are free.
    Justify our snapped chains, bless the black man.

God has closed His fist against those who would
    refuse His word, blood, love, what Nature requires

of Reason—yes, I read, as well you should—
    we will claim His rights, even to hellfire.

Felix! I'm unashamed to answer who-
    ever asks, *What man was sent to seed a family,*

snatch his birthright, demand life, joy and truth,
    liberty, religion, and property?

Felix! Quick or dead, here is a black man—
    the heir to great, struck blessings: free black man.

LEMUEL HAYNES, A FUTURE MINISTER,
A FORMERLY INDENTURED SERVANT, AND
SON OF AN ENGLISHWOMAN AND AFRICAN,
JOINS THE MINUTEMEN OF HIS TOWN

Granville, c. 1774

in death freedom   struck cheek the Heir's blessing
for the guilty   i will have none of that

prefer the Christ whose hum withers testing
eat the flesh   drink the blood   lay on faith's slat

i want a Savior with no tame *mercy*
to reveal men unshriven   my brethren

meek praying that freedom shall not disperse
and i fondle the old pages   swearing

blood   the Son's dame labored him   open eye
for the other   eye unsoothed   eye sinner

my mother gave me away   negro's child
a lonely life controlled   constant winter

i do not want love   an untested shout
and if these words offend thee   pluck me out

FRAGMENT #2: FIRST DRAFT OF AN EXTANT LETTER, ABIGAIL ADAMS, BOSTON, TO JOHN ADAMS, PHILADELPHIA

September 22, 1774

> ~~my dearest friend if words offend forgive~~
> There has been in Town a conspiracy
> of the Negroes. At present it is kept
> pretty private ~~you ignore my feelings~~
> ~~swatting needs to the skies i am taller~~
> ~~than wife~~ I wish most sincerely there was
> not a Slave in the province. It always
> appeard a most iniquitious Scheme to
> me — fight ourselfs for what we are daily
> robbing and plundering from those who have
> as good a right to freedom as we have.
> You know my mind upon this Subject. ~~i~~
> ~~have some damned rights too and if all of these~~
> ~~children didn't cling if i were a man~~ . . .

SALEM POOR FIGHTS AT THE
BATTLE OF BUNKER HILL

Charlestown, Boston, June 17, 1775

Liberty is a rage, man's designated
      right to shoot bullets at a nemesis.

It's not about stages, the creation
      of kings, their deeds, property, legacy.

When Salem Poor joined the pitiful caw
      of soldiers—though the nervous Washington

didn't want Negroes anywhere drawing
      iron—Salem wanted his name written

on somebody's lips, memory, paper.
      To shine with his free urgent brethren

who showed on this hill, too, sandpaper
      scraping southern colonists' fear and skin.

Across seas, Salem's kin (maybe) were free.
      Here they fought: dying, living. Either way, free.

FRAGMENT #3: FIRST DRAFT OF AN EXTANT LETTER, PHILLIS WHEATLEY, PROVIDENCE, TO GENERAL GEORGE WASHINGTON, CAMBRIDGE HEADQUARTERS

October 26, 1775

Sir, I have taken the freedom ~~which if
my master hadn't given me would have
been my own anyway~~ to address your
Excellency ~~who I heard behaves like
either a gentleman or a tyrant
depending on his moods or his money~~
in the enclosed poem ~~filled with desperate
attempts to prick your male vanity~~ and
entreat your acceptance ~~you should be glad
i wrote~~ though I am not insensible
~~of your cruel aversion to Negro
men who fight for the indefensible~~
Your Excellency's most obedient
Servant ~~this humility is tedious~~ . . .

LORD DUNMORE DECIDES TO OFFER FREEDOM TO SLAVES TO FIGHT IN SUPPORT OF HIS MAJESTY, KING GEORGE III

November 7, 1775

A tedious matter, that I must deal
    with rebels, these ungrateful landowners

fanning tall kites of sedition, whining heels
    calling themselves slaves: mark my loud laughter.

They know nothing of bondage, that someone
    has to be above and someone below.

There is the stranger, servant, or the son.—
    Now Negroes, now choose: which place will you go?

It might as well be you on Glory's knee.
    It might as well be you who I call free.

You can't win against the rock of power—
    break it to gravel: now it is a mountain.

It might as well be you who takes this chance.
    It might as well be you making bullets dance.

GENERAL GEORGE WASHINGTON ALLOWS THE ENLISTMENT OF FREE (THOUGH NOT ENSLAVED) NEGROES IN THE CONTINENTAL ARMY

Cambridge, December 30, 1775

What madness, niggers making bullets dance!
    In my life, I have never heard of such,

and I have traveled wide through this land,
    butchered Indians in Ohio, throats cut.

In my life, I have never heard of such,
    where wagons pull oxen, and rain makes clouds.

In Ohio, I killed, the blood flowed, throats cut—
    I'm supposed to salute niggers now?

What noise: wagons pulling oxen, rain making clouds,
    lunacy alchemied by Lord Dunmore.

I'm supposed to salute niggers now,
    live a new life, washed on my mother's shore?

I can't unsee the travails of this chance—
    what madness, niggers making bullets dance.

February 28, 1776

Her letter trembles in my hand, dances
    with confusion, swaying past the stars—

that she perched on fissures, such black chance:
    on those black cheeks are there pagan scars?

An African, a girl who wrote this poem,
    the hand graceful, the verse so stoked with praise

that I am consumed by clattering omen—
    bold, she wrote to me, none of my house slaves

would dare, would be allowed this presumption
    but northern men encourage the spilling

of ink by women and blacks, the gumption
    of those who serve and cost pound and shilling.

Her quill and life defy my age's Reason.
    She steps in God's house, a different season.

February–July 1776

Who lives in this House   a different season
        though the trees look the same   *what is the Name*

of the Head   instead death's overtaking
        you like a fool quick in love   *How many*

Persons in this house have had the Small Pox
        both white & black   sick africans   hopeful

black men   runaways   courageous strangers
        How many Persons belonging to this

family are now in the service   air
        assaults most everything   take your faith

take freedom   take your wife   your child   your eyes
        before it's done   *Is it Continental*

or Colonial   *if by sea in what*
        vessel & how many of each have died

AN ISSUE OF MERCY #3

African American soldiers at Valley Forge, 1777–1778

We are Washington's black vessels: *mercy*.
    In light, we tote our own long guns: *mercy*.

The ground here an abomination: snow
    tight packed, small fires, little food. No *mercy*.

How many of us brethren? At least five
    hundred Africans, a drum mind: *mercy*.

Our fight's not for rage only, and that ship
    remembers our bones, as do we: *mercy*.

But you, our children, discard quiet ones,
    spit *slave* at them. Tell us: where's *mercy*?

Like soldiers, those slaves bled, and they survived.
    They kept us—their children—alive: *mercy*.

We black men slipped from the ship's grasp. Breathing
    and bold, shooting. Is that not *mercy*?

HARRY WASHINGTON, A NEGRO RUNAWAY FORMERLY BELONGING TO GEORGE WASHINGTON, SAILS ON *L'ABONDENCE*, BOUND FOR PORT ROSEWAY, NOVA SCOTIA

City of New York, July 31, 1783

I'm free, I can breathe, a delicious *mercy.*
  I signed my name in the *Book of Negroes*—

In Canada, I'll farm, plant my own trees,
  green food and fruit in a strong woman's womb.

Jump the broom with that same lady I chose—
  Not bought by Master at the auction block

after he pawed her, told me, *Show*
  your teeth. Act glad. Lie with her. Don't back talk.

I was his own, but the war is over.
  I pray for a wife, to touch her wide hips

as we sway, dip around our homely stove,
  our children playing at the hearth's warm lip.

I sleep and grind my teeth, but I own them.
  I ran away before Master could pull them.

THE DEATH OF FORMER PRESIDENT GEORGE WASHINGTON

Mount Vernon, December 14, 1799

I bought and used slaves' teeth to chew my food—
    the truth: my people were afraid of me.

I'm dying: in that far corner, my good
    man clutches a chair, his pretense of grief

battling his nightmares, and behind him
    framed the dark ones that I promised freedom.

That would be the day I heard Death's toes click—
    I vowed to them, but do they pray over me,

that I won't die and leave their children sold?
    Mondays through Fridays and God-sent Sundays

my Negroes rose and worked before cock's crow.
    That man in the corner laid cloth on me, but what

can I know of his wait, the reverie
    of death: scattered kin, auctioned memory?

REVOLUTION: BLACK SORTIE, BLACK REDOUBLÉ

c. 1770–1783

scattered   auctioned kindred   claim them   black man

language of wounded throats   shout on   black man

glittered affray   come on with it   black man

don't you turn your cheek   strike for blood   black man

don't care for offense   pluck what's owed   black man

liberty is rage   take the stage   black man

take your freedom   take your chance   *oh*   black man

tedious battle but you can deal   black man

there's madness in bullets dancing   black man

your woman trembles but she prays   black man

a different season   ascend   black man

in good fighting   there is *mercy*   black man

you're free to live   to breathe   shine on   black man

grind your powder   hymn your life   sing   black man

Book: Liberty

I attended, and find exactly true your thoughts on the
behavior of those who seem'd to respect me while under
my mistresses patronage: you said right, for Some of those
have already put on a reserve . . .
— Letter from Phillis Wheatley to John Thornton,
    October 30, 1774

You will do me a great favour if you'll
write me by every Opp'y.—Direct your letters
under cover to Mr. John Peters in Queen Street . . .
— Letter from Phillis Wheatley to Obour Tanner,
    May 29, 1778

LOST LETTER #21: PHILLIS WHEATLEY, BOSTON, TO OBOUR TANNER, NEWPORT

March 13, 1778

Sister:

My master has died and sanctified his soul.
I did not expect him to last this long
after his bad fall and my dear mistress passing.

There was much suffering and when my
asthma came, I could not tend to him.

[my beloved told me stop calling the old man master
i've not been owned for years but the word
will not desert my lips my beloved is angry

my master did not leave me a pound or a shilling
i was a slave for twelve years an unpaid servant for five]

God's *mercy* on my master now!—
He was a gruff man, but never laid
his hand on me in strife.

There was no whip or stick, only a mere
nod when I completed a task.

[i am my own property and not nathaniel's a
woman of twenty-four with my own name master
did not give me that but he did not slap it away]

The truth too cloudy, that I was alone
and small that summer morning on the docks.

[my beloved knew his mother until she died he
cannot see my fears that any dear look is a bright
word from heaven why my affection is steadfast]

May God pull my master quickly into paradise.
Please say many prayers for him.

Your Phillis

....

The death of Mary Wheatley Lathrop, September 24, 1778

She married the minister:
life shadowed by Puritans,
women rivered by life.
This: the lot of wife.
But Phillis:
a logic of freedom.

This little light of mine
I'm gone let it shine

As in the song by Negro brethren
a bit later than this scene—
in germy, southern climes,
after Whitney's gin blots
out relative memory.
No Penicillin. No hygiene.
No aspirin,
only prayer and sinking.

This little light of mine
I'm gone let it shine

Mary's lap once held the little girl.
Her finger pointing out
female possibility: *Phillis,*
you own that word, as He owns you.
A wife's light now pricked.
God's call eclipsed.

Let it shine
Let it shine
Let it shine

October 12, 1778

Sister:

I've been rubbing chaff off seeds,
dreaming of the gold my mother wore
around her neck and in her ears. My father

gave this treasure when they married,
and she spoke to me of unions.

[i have no husband or gold and i am
not you i do not speak to important people
in many lands or conjure tongues and stories]

I wish you joy, if Mr. Peters is your choice—
but you have many other chances.

[i have heard the stories about that man
that he despises to work with his hands
how can he support you in this time of war]

Yet if you are of a praying mind, meditate
on your long life ahead as wife.

Will you not reconsider Master Thornton's
proposal to sail back across the water and give
your hand to either of those African missionaries?

[i have heard john peters does not pay attention
in church that he wishes to rise above his birth]

If you are ever in need of a bed,
please travel to me in Newport.
I am yet a slave, but you are my kin.

[i have heard you are sinning with that man
is he even trying to fight as a soldier]

Your Obour

AFTER LIVING TOGETHER FOR SEVERAL MONTHS, PHILLIS WHEATLEY AND JOHN PETERS, FREE NEGROES, ARE MARRIED BY THE REVEREND JOHN LATHROP, WIDOWER OF MARY WHEATLEY LATHROP

Second Church, Boston, November 26, 1778

Let them walk home
from church, naughty
and able.
Let John's poet-woman
take off that damned, dainty cap.
Let him worship
her exquisite body of naps.
Let them descend to the bed—
again—
for the fiftieth or hundredth time.
The Devil take these preachers
giving advice
on obedient slaves.
If John and Phillis already
praised in an unblessed room,
if the ground congregated
under four sinful feet, jumping
over an unseen broom?
They are *Free Negroes*
and I'm leaving now—
they need privacy—
but I can taste
their fruit, what the birds
fought me for.
What more?
Amen.
Give them this.

PHILLIS PETERS PREPARES A PROPOSAL TO PUBLISH A SECOND BOOK

c. October 15, 1779

All her Wheatleys have left her
or have died, and besides,
during the War, she is poor.
Really poor: the last name of *Peters*
pays no debts and bakes no bread.
New England is destitute.
                 (Did you think that because
                     of Revolution, white
         men would give
             rights to Negroes?
                Or suddenly, lift up
        their own, white wives?
           I know.
              I, too, have my hopes
             about power subsiding.
        It is human
           to expect that
             in a flick of a quill,
       a lost paradise
         will beckon.)
Behold the Negro Poetess,
she that once clung to stone.
Turned now: a discarded rock.
Yet, Phillis Peters still
knows her fine mind,
the *sable* genius turning
on words.

BLUES: IN THE SMALL ROOM
WHERE HE LIVES WITH HIS WIFE

John Peters, Boston, c. 1784

There's a chair occupied by Phillis,
his love who trembles & prays
for her John to be relieved of debt.
Phillis clasping his promise
to *make it all right* despite his Negro's
lot in the time after Revolution.

After supposed liberty, John's war
to feed himself & his Phillis,
to be more than a poor Negro
searching for money, praying
for God to fulfill Heaven's promise.
But on earth, nothing but debt.

In Boston, way too much debt.
The colonies needed coins for war,
their white man's freedom, their promises.—
In the meantime, a coughing Phillis.
In the meantime, John's praying
to be more than a broke Negro.

On the streets, other brothers,
thin, looking hopeless, battling debt.—
On the streets: plenty praying.
On the cobblestones, the war's
deficit, hunger at home: Phillis,
sick but smiling, speaking vows

she made the day she married, promises
given to her free, smart Negro—
John, man of ideas, joined with Phillis,
woman of words, but the truth is debt
left by Revolution. A costly war.
The truth is starving & praying.

The truth: a sinking boat & praying
not to drown, to fulfill intention.
The truth is this land's Revolution
wasn't waged for the black man's
or black woman's right to freedom: debt
is owed to our coughing poetess—

to my people battling freedom's prayer—
& Phillis is wrapped in John's promises.
Her love, her man trembles with debt.

SEARCHING FOR YEARS BUT FAILING TO FIND DOCUMENTATION THAT PHILLIS WHEATLEY (PETERS) ACTUALLY GAVE BIRTH TO THREE CHILDREN WHO DIED IN INFANCY OR EARLY CHILDHOOD

If there were children

    & how many children

If they were born

    & were they called to God

If there were headstones

    & a black mother weeping

If Phillis rocked them

    & how would you know

If there were children

    & would that give you joy

If they had names

    & three beloveds died

If there weren't children

    & would that give you joy

If they were baptized

    & where is the *mercy*

If they coughed & bled

    & they perished in song

If like their mother

    & they cried for home

If they reached water

    & would that give you joy

If there was mourning

    & Sisters weeping

If they were called

    & what is this called

If they sang home

    & what kind of mourning

If there is truth

    & what has truth been

LOST LETTER #23: PHILLIS PETERS, BOSTON, TO OBOUR TANNER, NEWPORT

October 12, 1784

Dear Sister:

I ask your forgiveness: it has been a sharp
spell since I have written, and I was wrong to leave
you with no word. I am sorry to say my John

is imprisoned in Boston-Gaol, yet I'm
grateful to live with Mistress's old friends.

[white men took my husband for a debt
they came to our room and beat on the door
i begged him to climb out the window

but he refused he said he was no coward
he could not abide speaking in whispers

he lives now in boston-gaol without his
care i have begun to cough again at night
i am trapped by charity my hosts remember

when i was a slave i cannot tell them
i was always free in the cleft of gambia

it was not your place to ask me to forget john
i know there is nothing wrong with a man's
bleeding knuckles with hands that know labor

our Lord was a carpenter but john works from
his mouth and head and sister he is so kind]

It rains, and poesy is dear and spare.
I contemplate soldier-brethren, how their
families are starving after their deeds of war.

My stone, I am your kin from ever,
Phillis

LOST LETTER #24: PHILLIS PETERS, BOSTON, TO JOHN PETERS, BOSTON-GAOL

November 19, 1784

My Beloved Husband

I wait for word from you, and tend
to my duties for my benefactors.
I thank the Savior that my mistress's

wings in Heaven have provided me
with a free fire and room and food.

*[i dream of children we have never raised
i dream of breasts never filled leaking
into absent mouths in my sleep there are hands*

*pinching my skirts and i worry over cries
and trifles this woman misses you she who*

*would have eaten coals for her greatest
and only love i am here in someone else's home
witnessing the evidence of emptiness my days*

*reconciled to imagination and coughing
i cannot believe you are in that place again]*

I pray that you are keeping from the cold.
I send a poem, my affection, and always
my admiration, wherever you may be.

Your wife,
Phillis

LOST LETTER #25: JOHN PETERS, BOSTON-GAOL, TO PHILLIS PETERS, BOSTON

November 30, 1784

My Sweet Wife,

Please write your man and touch my care.
There is no need for fear, for no one dares
to read your letters: we are Negroes and poor.

No one awaits to take our love and spin ink
on a broadside. Please don't fill with temper.

I should have written sooner, but paper
and ink are scarce, and I could not think
of what I might do to secure the means.

*[i have never been on a ship but
these jailors bear the look of sailors*

*they are greedy to touch offer terrible prices
and i want to come home to you clean be
patient with me woman oh let me be clean]*

Phillis, please write. I hope your silence
only means anger and that you do not cough.

I wait each day for news.
I told the men in this heaving cell that
you are the famed Negro Poetess.

They laughed until your first favor arrived
and then I read your lines to them.

[i am still your good man i have tried woman
don't you understand i love you i have tried
surely you know i have tried there was no

money after the war everyone was starving
but i gave my meals to you i have tried]

Christmas is coming
and snow will drift through these bars.
Please send a poem my way, as

your words are my only want.
My love, I need to know you are alive.

Your John

Epilogue: Daughter/Muse

> Fortunately for black women . . . some powerful
> new truths had begun to emerge, truths which
> forced a new space to accommodate the very
> telling of them. All of this, we owe to Phillis
> Wheatley.
> — Margaret Walker, "Phillis Wheatley
>   and Black Women Writers, 1773–1973"

> To conclude on a personal note, this has been
> a painful book to write, and if I have done any
> justice to the subject, it will be a painful book
> to read. There is no way around this, nor should
> there be.
> — Marcus Rediker, *The Slave Ship: A Human History*

HOMEGOING, OR, THE CROSSING OVER OF GOONAY, LATELY KNOWN AS PHILLIS PETERS

Boston, December 5, 1784

The journey is over
but I can—*shall*—answer:

Yes, even here.
Even in this small, cluttered room

in a house in a city in a place
I cannot leave.

Even *there*—on that long-ago ship,
the planks slick with mourning—

before my name was changed,
and I awoke on this side of water:

God.

Whatever song of whatever prayer,
and that bird in the air following

that vessel of dying children—
what a miracle her flight!

Those filigreed bones beneath
the thin blood blanket,

that too-new heart bruised by cries.
Long ago, but surely a *mercy*—

            (there is a spot

                   in the ditch

       of my mind

                grass

     growing

                over the graves
            where

       the

          children
          are buried

 oh

       I cannot

            find it
         this
        a blessing

                 too
         that bird
       has eaten

                  the trail

      leading

          to that
            place)

Wake up, Yaay.

Come to the doorway
and call a prayer
to me.

LOOKING FOR MISS PHILLIS[1]

As a little girl in the 1970s, for Black History Month I memorized the names of prominent African Americans, whose images my teachers would trace on construction paper, then tack to the bulletin boards in my school. How I loved those dark silhouettes.

My school was ninety-nine percent black, de facto segregated; the laws had changed in the South, but custom had not. My teachers celebrated black "firsts" to shore up our self-esteem, to fortify us against our smaller and shabbier schools and a pervasive white unfriendliness from those outside our enclave. To my teachers, the eighteenth-century poet Phillis Wheatley was the *first* of the firsts, a beacon for black children.

My parents were teachers, too: professors. My father was on the tenure track, my mother an adjunct, and at home they filled in the details on Phillis Wheatley. She was a child stolen from across the Atlantic and enslaved. A young genius whose playthings were the poems of Homer and Terence, she was the first African woman on this side of the Atlantic to publish a book of poetry. Neither of my parents liked (or respected) her poetry much, but that wasn't the point. The point was loyalty to the race, to African American men and women. This probably wasn't my first lesson about the responsibilities of being a black person, but it's the first one I remember and the most lasting.

I don't recall my elementary school teachers or my parents ever mentioning Wheatley's husband. I believed then that she never had married before dying at the young age of around thirty or thirty-one, and I found it heartbreaking that she did not have someone to love from her native land, someone who looked like her and shared the same cultural memories. All she had was the white people who used to own her.

When I first encountered unofficial information about Wheatley's husband, John Peters, in my junior year of college, I was confronted with the dominant negative stereotypes of black men. My African American literature professor's words described him as an arrogant good-for-nothing who deserted his family. Talladega College, where I was studying at the time, was founded in 1867 by formerly enslaved African Americans. The campus is situated in a rural Alabama town, but smack in the middle of the 'hood.

When I considered how John Peters was portrayed by my professor, how he had abandoned Phillis and their three children, leaving them to poverty and then eventual death in the midst of squalor, images of other black men came to me: the shiftless brothers who hung at the edge of campus, townies waiting for college girls. They sometimes shouted to us and promised pleasures of all kinds. These were the young men my doggedly middle-class mother had warned me about, in her cigarette-tuned alto voice. My mother had fought her way up from backwoods poverty in rural Georgia and she cautioned me: One wrong step with a man could land me in perdition, living in a shack or a one-room apartment surrounded by my screaming, misbehaving progeny. As a formerly poor person, my mother looked down her nose at poor black folk who had not escaped to tell the advisory tale, as she had.

I thought of Phillis, the "Ethiop" genius, taken in by John's charms and falling from her magnificent perch. I pictured her beguiled by a man who whispered in her ear, told her lies to get into her starched, Good Negro bloomers.

But I never really considered her as this man's wife.

. . . .

Much of the information on Phillis Wheatley's personal life comes from *Memoir and Poems of Phillis Wheatley, A Native African and a Slave*, a book published in 1834, fifty years after the poet's death. The one named as author of the book, Margaretta Matilda Odell, is identified as a relative of Susannah Wheatley: "Lastly, the author of this Memoir is a collateral descendant of Mrs. Wheatley, and has been familiar with the name and fame of Phillis from her childhood."[2] Odell pushes a well-meaning anti-slavery message: black folks do not deserve to be in chains, and someone like Wheatley is the example of what other African Americans could achieve, if they only had a chance.

According to Odell, the child who would be renamed Phillis was "supposed to have been about seven years old, at this time, from the circumstance of shedding her front teeth," when she arrived in Boston harbor.[3] Susannah Wheatley, the wife of a merchant, was looking for a "faithful domestic in her old age."[4] Instead, she found "the poor, naked child" with a piece of cloth tied around her like a skirt.[5] Once the child was taken home,

> A daughter of Mrs. Wheatley, not long after the child's first
> introduction to the family, undertook to learn her to read and write;

and, while she astonished her instructress by her rapid progress, she won the good will of her kind mistress, by her amiable disposition and the propriety of her behavior.[6]

As a biographer, Odell paints the white Wheatleys as kind masters, and draws an especially sympathetic portrait of Susannah. With the help of her mistress, the smart and well-behaved enslaved slave child began writing poetry, and Susannah acted as an eighteenth-century stage mother to push forward her charge's poetry career.[7] Odell doesn't give specific dates for Phillis Wheatley's eventual journey to freedom, but later biographers of the poet do, such as Vincent Carretta, author of *Phillis Wheatley: Biography of a Genius in Bondage*. Carretta writes that on May 8, 1773, she sailed to London (accompanied by the Wheatleys' grown son, Nathaniel) to promote her work, staying there six weeks.[8] On September 9, 1773, advertisements appeared for Wheatley's only published book of poetry, *Poems on Various Subjects, Religious and Moral*.[9] We know that upon her return from London, her owners freed her, because Wheatley mentions this fact in a letter to David Wooster dated October 18, 1773.[10]

Susannah Wheatley wrote to Selena Hastings, Countess of Huntingdon, a philanthropist and a leader in the Methodist movement, in an attempt to secure her patronage for the young poet.[11] And Phillis herself wrote lovingly of Susannah in a letter to her African American friend Obour Tanner, describing how the white woman treated Phillis as less a "servant" and more a "child."[12] As we look back on this era, however, the kindness of the Wheatleys must be viewed through a complex prism, for slavery was a scatological, morally bankrupt enterprise. Vincent Carretta writes that, besides Phillis, the Wheatleys owned at least one other slave.[13] There are no public records of them raising their voices publicly or acting overtly against the institution of slavery. Odell seems to think that Phillis was living the kidnapped African's dream, however, and that, after the death of Susannah, that dream collapsed:

> At this period of destitution, Phillis received an offer of marriage from a respectable colored man of Boston. The name of this individual was Peters. He kept a grocery in Court-Street, and was a man of very handsome person and manners; wore a wig, carried a cane, and quite acted out "the gentleman." In an evil hour he was accepted; and he proved utterly unworthy of the distinguished woman who honored

him by her alliance. He was unsuccessful in business, and failed soon after their marriage; and he is said to have been both too proud and too indolent to apply himself to any occupation below his fancied dignity. Hence his unfortunate wife suffered much from this ill-omened union.[14]

The truths in Odell's *Memoir and Poems of Phillis Wheatley* are mixed in with undocumented speculations, as well as outright falsehoods, especially when it came to Peters. For example, Odell informs us that Wheatley never used the last name of her husband—and, it's implied, we should assume that this decision had something to do with Peters's qualities as a mate. This is untrue: in a 1779 letter to Obour Tanner, the poet signs herself as "Phillis Peters"; thereafter, with rare exceptions, she uses her married name.[15] Having written in great, flattering detail about the poet's years with the white Wheatleys, Odell uses her talents to draw a contemptuous likeness of John Peters. Odell accuses him of possible abuse, writing in delicate terms that while Phillis Wheatley was in very bad health, she wouldn't have been "unmindful . . . of her conjugal or matronly duties."[16] In other words, Peters pressed his frail wife into sexual service when he shouldn't have, which resulted in (according to Odell) three pregnancies.

From there, Odell opines, Wheatley's destruction was a foregone conclusion. There was terrible poverty. Each of the three children born to Wheatley fell sick in infancy and died. And at the age of thirty or thirty-one, Wheatley herself died from an illness exacerbated by her "extreme misery" in living in "a filthy apartment" with a "negligent" husband.[17] Odell writes that Peters "demanded" his late wife's papers from her white friends, but as Wheatley's widower and next of kin, that certainly would have been Peters's right.[18]

It is unclear why Odell was so antagonistic toward Peters, or why, if her charges against him as a "negligent" husband were true, she would have felt the need to embellish those truths with glaring falsehoods. It seems simple to accuse Odell of racism, but she is very sympathetic toward Wheatley. Thus, we know that Odell is no raving, anti-black individual, but taken with her outright lies about John Peters, confusion on her motives for writing a book on Phillis Wheatley prevails.

In 2003, I read an essay written by Henry Louis Gates Jr. in the *New Yorker*, an excerpt from his soon-to-be-published book, *The Trials of Phillis Wheatley: America's First Black Poet and Her Encounters with the Founding Fathers*, a treatment of Wheatley juxtaposed against the racism of Enlightenment scholars such as Immanuel Kant and more specifically Thomas Jefferson, who had criticized Wheatley's poetry as "below the dignity of criticism."[19] As someone who had explored American history in my poetry, I found Gates's thesis fascinating: He believed Wheatley was important in dispelling derisive eighteenth-century notions about black humanity; her poetry had rebutted Kant's ordering of the nations with Africans down at the very bottom. Wheatley became an important symbol for black humanity.[20]

My encounter with Gates's article started me on a reading jag about Wheatley. For the next six years, I read everything I could find on her. I checked books out from the library, such as Katherine Clay Bassard's moving, scholarly treatment of Wheatley (and other black women), *Spiritual Interrogations: Culture, Gender and Community in Early African American Women's Writing*. I downloaded scholarly articles, and I began to think deeply about Wheatley's most (in)famous poem, "On Being Brought from Africa to America":

'Twas mercy brought me from my Pagan land,
Taught my benighted soul to understand
That there's a God, that there's a Saviour too:
Once I redemption neither sought nor knew.
Some view our sable race with scornful eye,
"Their colour is a diabolic die."
Remember, Christians, Negros, black as Cain,
May be refin'd, and join th' angelic train.

This eight-line poem begins with discordancy, with seeming racial self-hatred combined with religious fervor. The tone of these verses earned Wheatley sharp, ugly criticism from later black poets, most notably the Black Arts Movement poet Amiri Baraka (né LeRoi Jones).[21] As a woman in my (then) thirties, I had a different take from Baraka's. I thought about a little girl's pain at being torn from her parents in Africa, and her trauma on board a slave ship. I thought of her mother's grief, wondering what had become of her child. I thought about my own and other black folks' beliefs in a benevolent God, in spite of our history in this country, and the brutality enacted against us.

However, until I traveled to Worcester, Massachusetts, to the American Antiquarian Society, I had no idea that the devastating picture of the naked, gap-toothed child wrapped in a carpet may have been Odell's imaginary reflection.

It was 2009, and I was the recipient of a Creative and Performing Artists and Writers fellowship at the Society, whose archives house one of the largest collections of printed material about the United States, the West Indies, and Canada from early colonial days through 1876. I was on a mission to write a series of poems based upon Phillis Wheatley's life, and I was in search of primary sources.

At the beginning of my fellowship, I was ready to get to work. Though I'd been conducting archival research on African Americans for nearly twenty years, I wasn't formally trained as a historian, and yet as the research librarians remarked, I was quick and a self-starter. In only a matter of days, I found references to Odell's *Memoir and Poems of Phillis Wheatley*. Looking through the bibliographies in texts on Wheatley, I noticed that they either cited Odell directly or they summarized Odell and listed a "relative" of the Wheatley family as a reference. However, there was no overt tracing of Odell's lineage, no documented proof of exactly how she was related to the Wheatleys. No way to establish Odell's authority.

In July, around the middle of my fellowship term, I drove from Worcester to the National Archives at Boston (actually located in Waltham, Massachusetts). It was at the urging of Caroline Sloat, my mentor at the Society, that I made the drive, even after she told me that records would be on microfiche, the very mention of which made me sick to my stomach. I spent a couple hours looking through the census records, and as I feared, it was not the exhilarating process I'd hoped for. My eyeballs ached and the lobster roll from the day before threatened to repeat on me.

I was ready to return to Worcester, when I saw a "John Peters" on the 1790 census of Suffolk County, Massachusetts—the city of Boston. He was listed as a free man of color.

No, it wasn't a mistake. There was his name.

Swallowing my nausea, I rechecked the entire census, just to be sure. There was no other African American "John Peters," the supposedly narcissistic man who had abandoned his wife off and on, and then—as Odell had written—moved south after his wife's death. I looked the census over completely two more times and took pictures of the relevant pages.

Then I sat there, confused. Rather than verifying facts about America's first black poet, which had been my intention, I realized literary history had entrusted the story of Phillis Wheatley and John Peters to a white woman who may have made assumptions about Wheatley's husband, assumptions that might not just be wrong, but also the product of racial stereotypes. Such as, why *would* Peters have moved farther south after the Revolution? This piece of the mystery had never made sense to me. Why would a *free* black man in his natural right mind move south, taking his body to slaveholding territory, where white men probably would be waiting to place him in chains?

Wheatley had died in 1784, but the census I was looking at was taken six years later, which meant that Peters might have been in Boston when his wife passed away. What could this mean? Had the couple been separated? Had he left her for another woman or man? Had she left him? Or had they remained together? Maybe he hadn't abandoned her. Maybe Odell had misrepresented their relationship. And if Odell had misrepresented the relationship of Wheatley and Peters, maybe she had done the same about Phillis Wheatley's relationship to the white Wheatleys—maybe I should have been viewing Odell's biography with skepticism.

As a black, female poet whose career was made possible by the accomplishments of Phillis Wheatley, I was not only curious about her life, but also, curious how it intersected with the lives of other African Americans.

Odell's biography of Phillis Wheatley does not truly address the pre-slavery life of the poet. Other than repeatedly using the word "African" as a vehicle for what appears to be anti-slavery sentiment, Odell ignores Wheatley's homeland. And other than two scant references to Wheatley's mother, who "poured out water before the sun at his rising," there are no references to Wheatley's parents, either.[22] Her father is not mentioned overtly, and Odell tells us that the enslaved child forgot her early life and, it is assumed, her African language. The implication is that this child was a blank—though *black*—slate, upon which Susannah Wheatley could write her own intentions. After Odell's short and rather vague discussion about Phillis Wheatley's Middle Passage journey, that experience is discarded too. Her enslaved existence is described as idyllic, as if she were isolated from her traumatic displacement, ignored other African Americans who'd come across the Atlantic, embraced whiteness as superior, and happily situated herself within a white household and elite white social, religious, and literary circles.

I found these ancestral and cultural lacunae in Odell's biography deeply troubling. While we can't know if Wheatley longed for her African homeland after receiving her freedom, if she did not want to return, there would have been a reason. She would have risked being recaptured and resold into slavery. We do know that she retained a connection to the continent and its people, for she developed a years-long friendship with Obour Tanner, another enslaved African woman. Wheatley wrote fervently spiritual letters to Tanner, and we can presume that Tanner included the same sorts of sentiments in her own correspondence. (There are no extant letters by Tanner, however.) This friendship should have presented glaring challenges to Wheatley's supposed anti-blackness, and to that pesky "House Negro" narrative about Wheatley, one that has prevailed for many years.

Further, this narrative about a "privileged" Wheatley is grossly illogical, for no matter the so-called kindness of white masters or white benefactors, black slavery *or* black freedom in the Americas never could equal the privilege of eighteenth-century whiteness. And when considering that Wheatley was an enslaved *woman* maintaining a friendship with another enslaved woman, we should know that intersectional realities would have complicated Wheatley's so-called privilege all the more.

Though Odell provides our earliest and most lasting depiction of the poet's life, thus far Vincent Carretta's *Phillis Wheatley: Biography of a Genius in Bondage* is the most comprehensive biography of the poet. Still, even Carretta doesn't discuss Wheatley's pre-slavery existence. Like most other Wheatley biographers, he begins his treatment of her at the Boston Harbor in 1761, with her disembarking a slave ship. This anecdote describes Wheatley seven or eight years after her birth, and Carretta's rare references to Africa are entangled with the Transatlantic Slave Trade. There are no prolonged passages about West African culture or about Wheatley's African parents, and Carretta doesn't do much to connect Wheatley to African American quotidian existence. Yet we must give Carretta credit for his devotion to Wheatley, for he has carefully unearthed a treasure trove of material on her—and on John Peters and Obour Tanner. Within *Phillis Wheatley: Biography of a Genius in Bondage*, there are legal documents, newspaper notices, and records in Boston's *Taking Book*, along with other essential minutiae.

Though Carretta used Odell's biography as an account by a (white) Wheatley relative, he did point out some falsehoods in the biography.[23] And he discusses Revolutionary-era Boston, documenting Wheatley's life in the years leading up to the war and directly afterward. It is easy to imagine that African American figures of this era would have captured Wheatley's attention, for she wrote a poem about the Boston Massacre.[24] Just as I had heard the name of Phillis Wheatley in elementary school, so had I learned about Crispus Attucks, a biracial African-Indigenous man, and the first to fall in the Massacre. Over the years, I would learn the names of others, including Lemuel Haynes, a minister who had fought in the Revolution. I would read the words of Felix, an unidentified black man—and presumably a slave—who petitioned the Massachusetts General Court in 1773, demanding his freedom and that of other African American men.[25] But the activist who intrigued me the most was Belinda Sutton, whose 1783 petition to the Court asked for an old age pension to support herself and her disabled daughter, a legacy that had been provided in her former master's will. Sutton gives a moving account of her capture into slavery, as well as a moral indictment of slavery:

> [S]he realized, that Europeans placed their happiness in the yellow dust which she carelessly marked with her infant footsteps—even when she, in a sacred grove, with each hand in that of a tender Parent, was paying her devotions to the great Orisa who made all things— an armed band of white men, driving many of her Countrymen in Chains, ran into the hallowed shade![26]

What is especially striking here is that Sutton mentions that she was worshipping "the Orisa"—West African deities—when she was stolen. She must have been aware of her audience, but she boldly inserts this reference to African religion in her petition, knowing that the deciders of her case would be Christian.

Though Phillis Wheatley was a Christian as well, she fits in quite easily with these daring acts of rhetorical subversion by her African American brethren and sistren. Certainly, "On Being Brought from Africa to America" has influenced how most readers perceive Wheatley, but there are other poems that illustrate an embrace of her Africanness, such as "Philis's Reply to the Answer in Our Last by the Gentleman in the Navy," which describes her West African home as "pleasing Gambia."[27] And there is "To the Right Honorable William, Earl of Dartmouth," which contains lines about her possibly violent capture into slavery:

> I, young in life, by seeming cruel fate
> Was snatch'd from Afric's fancy'd happy seat:
> What pangs excruciating must molest,
> What sorrows labour in my parent's breast?
> Steel'd was that soul and by no misery mov'd
> That from a father seiz'd his babe belov'd:
> Such, such my case. And can I then but pray
> Others may never feel tyrannic sway?

Wheatley was a brilliant, insightful young woman. Surely, she must have known that these eight lines about her forced separation from her parents would greatly discomfit her white English and American readers, many of whom might have owned slaves themselves. Similar to Sutton's strongly worded petition, Wheatley's use of "tyrannic" serves as a moral indictment of slaveholders—and possibly even her own master and mistress.

Wheatley's choice of her own marriage mate—a free African American man—sent a symbolic statement as well. We know that in 1778, Phillis Wheatley and John Peters, "free Negroes," married during an especially tumultuous period of the American Revolution.[28] John Peters was a self-reliant individual. Carretta depicts him as a smart, hard worker, trying his hand in different business enterprises: law, commerce, real estate, even medicine.[29] (The latter was not the profession that we know today and required no specific schooling.) Peters wasn't afraid of whites, not in the least, which fits in with the black male revolutionary spirit of that era. Although there are no records of Peters fighting in the war, Carretta does document that Peters actually sued whites for money he felt was due him.[30] Given the racist attitudes—and, many times, violent actions—toward African Americans of the eighteenth century, Peters's moxie can only be called extraordinary.

As a white woman of the nineteenth century, Odell fits in perfectly with her era, too. It doesn't take much speculation to deduce that she believed John Peters to be an uppity Negro who convinced Wheatley—a privileged, well-behaved black woman—to discard her white friends. Odell believes that this departure led to Wheatley's eventual destruction: her tone ridicules Peters's ambitions, contending that he was "said to have been both too proud and too indolent to apply himself to any occupation below his fancied dignity."[31] In other words, how dare a black man want to be anything other than a day laborer with calluses on his hands? Who did he think he was, to desire property and not *be* property, to style himself as a business owner, to marry a high-status, accomplished woman, even if she was of his own race? However, there aren't any opinions on who Wheatley should have married. Though at the time Odell wrote her book, white women were expected to marry and bear children, Odell doesn't seem to have those same domestic expectations for Wheatley.

There are other second- or third-hand, similarly derisive accounts of John Peters, all by whites. Carretta's biography quotes from Josiah Quincy, who claims to have met John Peters in court, and who didn't think much of the encounter.[32] While doing my own research, I found a footnote in the November 1863 *Proceedings of the Massachusetts Historical Society*, in which the editors wrote that an acquaintance of Obour Tanner told someone else that Tanner had told her—keep up, now; this is getting complicated—that Tanner did not like Peters, that Wheatley had "let herself down" by marrying him.[33] But this same footnote giving ostensibly inside information also gets Wheatley's death date wrong, by ten years.

Odell claims that Phillis gave birth to children who died in infancy, though at this writing, there are no records for any children for the Peters family, no baptismal or burial documentation. If they did have children, like other black and white parents of the eighteenth century they would have worried about their offspring surviving. Infant mortality rates were disturbingly high during this period. It was not uncommon for black— or white—parents to lose several offspring in infancy or childhood; even those parents who fed, clothed, and loved their children. There would have been nothing Peters could have done to forestall a child's death from a disease such as measles.

As for whether Peters had a direct or indirect hand in Wheatley's death, there is no proof that he was abusive or caused her early death. In the eighteenth century, life spans were short for whites, and even shorter for African Americans. Wheatley suffered from asthma, and died around the age of thirty-one. Such an early death is difficult for us to absorb emotionally, but in the eighteenth century, unfortunately, thirty-one was the average life expectancy for black women in America.[34]

Carretta supplies evidence that, at the time of Wheatley's death, Peters was living in Massachusetts indeed, but he was likely in prison because he couldn't pay his bills.[35] In twenty-first-century terms, Peters had bad credit. This is not a crime by our contemporary standards, but it was in eighteenth-century New England. In the aftermath of the American Revolution, there was an economic depression in the former colonies.[36] Eventually, Peters was released from jail, and, according to Carretta, for the next sixteen years, he continued to aspire to the role of gentleman.[37]

There is proof that he kept trying to publish the second book of poetry that his late wife had written. On October 23, 2015, I corresponded by e-mail with Ashley Cataldo, assistant curator of manuscripts at the American Antiquarian Society. Knowing my interest in the Wheatley-Peters marriage, she shared with me an unpublished excerpt of a little-known letter (held by the Society) sent from the printer Ebenezer T. Andrews to his colleague Isaiah Thomas:

> I inclose you a Proposal Richards drew up for Wheatley's Poems. I told Peters that we would print them, at a certain price to be agreed upon (if sufficient subscribers appeared) and [after?] ourselves for printing, binding, +c. would divide the neat profits with him, which he consented . . .[38]

This proposal for a second book had been sent out by Wheatley before her death.[39] But bewilderingly, that book never was published. Carretta discovered that Peters died in 1801; he was around fifty-five at the time of his death.[40] Peters never was able to pay off his debts, but he did leave some nice belongings behind. A horse, a desk, some leather-bottomed chairs. Books, which meant he not only was literate, but may also have enjoyed reading.

When you look at Peters's life, okay, the brother "did a couple bids," but at least he didn't leave behind any *people* that had to be sold to erase his debts, as slaveholders such as Thomas Jefferson did. Enslaved African American families were broken up, auctioned off, and sifted like chaff: this would be the fate of the slaves of Monticello after Jefferson died.[41]

. . . .

That summer day in 2009, when I saw John Peters's name on the 1790 Suffolk County Census, I drove back from the National Archives to Worcester and huddled with Caroline Sloat and the research librarian at the American Antiquarian Society, Elizabeth Watts Pope. I asked them what Odell meant in her "Introduction" to *Memoir and Poems of Phillis Wheatley*, when she claimed to be a "collateral descendant" of the white Wheatleys: A cousin? A niece? An in-law married to a descendant of the Wheatley family? Both of them advised me to look up Odell on the New England Historic Genealogical Society database. I did, and I found Margaretta Matilda Odell of "Jamaica Plain, Massachusetts." And that's all I found.

I returned to searching through the primary-source texts on Phillis Wheatley; for example, I read through William H. Robinson's *Phillis Wheatley in the Black American Beginnings*; David C. Shields's *Phillis Wheatley's Poetics of Liberation: Background and Contexts*; and Vincent Carretta's "Introduction" to his edited *Complete Writings* of Phillis Wheatley. (Carretta's full biography of Wheatley had not yet been published.) In each, I double-checked the notes and indexes several times, sure that I must have overlooked something. Every night, back in my fellow's room, I took hours to draft possible genealogies of the blood relatives and in-laws of Susannah and John Wheatley, and those of their twin children, Mary Wheatley Lathrop and Nathaniel Wheatley. I uncovered no documentation connecting Odell to the white Wheatleys. There was no establishment of family bona fides. It appeared to me that the only proof that Odell had been related to Susannah Wheatley, the former mistress of Phillis Wheatley, was that *Odell had said so.*

When I returned home from Massachusetts to Oklahoma (where I have lived since 2002), I continued my research on Wheatley—whom I insisted on calling Phillis Wheatley *Peters*, considering that she discarded the surname of her former slave master and decided to take her husband's last name. I regularly searched for more information; I read new articles about her, and always I checked the source notes and bibliographies. Periodically, I looked for primary materials to see if any new information on her had emerged. When finances permitted, I traveled and conducted my research in person. In May 2012, I traveled to Senegal to become acquainted with the Wolof culture (and met and eventually married a Senegalese man, but that's another story for another essay). And in December 2013, I flew to England to trace (what I imagined to be) the steps of Wheatley Peters in London.

I had fallen in love with Phillis Wheatley Peters and I wanted to do right by her legacy. In 2010, I published an essay in *Commonplace: the journal of early American life* about the absence of documentation on Odell, arguing that scholars should renew the search for her genealogy:

Given the lack of documentation for Odell's family link to the white Wheatleys and the lack of proof for most of her assertions about Wheatley's life, it is distressing that, in 176 years, scholars have not questioned Odell's right to speak for Phillis Wheatley. This blind trust continues the disturbing historical trend of African Americans, and black women in particular, needing white benefactors to justify their lives and history.

In 2016, I published another essay in *The Fire This Time: A New Generation Speaks on Race*. Again I was hopeful, but there never was a seismic shift in Wheatley research. Scholars kept using Odell's *Memoir* as a reliable biographical text, although at conferences on Early American Studies, I kept repeating what I viewed as the problem: If no family records linking Odell to the white Wheatleys could be located, then the responsible, professional cause of action would be to cease using Odell as a primary source for Wheatley Peters's life. The other option would be to categorize *Memoir and Poems of Phillis Wheatley* as historical fiction, but whatever the categorization, I insisted, someone should challenge Odell's authority to provide the most enduring depiction of Wheatley Peters as a sycophant, and of her husband John as a hustler.

. . . .

Fast forward to June 2019, several days before the deadline to turn in this book to my publisher.

Those moments when you finish a book always are fraught with stress, with the fear that some huge mistake or glaring typo will appear in the book upon publication, after it is much too late to make any corrections. I sat in front of my computer, proofreading carefully, and yes, I found typos, but I encountered something more, something I hadn't paid enough attention to, in all these years.

When I went back to the November 1863 *Proceedings of the Massachusetts Historical Society*, to that footnote mentioning that Obour Tanner supposedly had criticized John Peters as a marriage mate for her friend, I saw a mention of Odell's *Memoir and Poems of Phillis Wheatley*, which gives the "facts" about Wheatley Peters's life "derived from grand-nieces of Phillis's benefactor, who are still living and corroborated by a grand-daughter of that lady, now residing in Boston."[42] Yet again, no names of those particular relatives were mentioned in this note—and as I kept reading, I encountered a reference to *another* "memoir" on Phillis Wheatley Peters, published in the *same* city and year—Boston, 1834—and by the *same* publisher, George W. Light. Only this time, the author was given as someone named B. B. Thatcher.[43] *Another* detail I hadn't paid enough attention to, for scholar Julian Mason had mentioned B. B. Thatcher's *Memoir* in *The Poems of Phillis Wheatley*. I remembered when I had read that reference. (Or rather, I remember when I read past it.)[44]

In the same way that I was struck to the bone by my encountering of the name of the supposedly absent, moved-south John Peters on the Suffolk County 1790 census, I was struck by the coincidence of this second biography of Phillis Wheatley by another author, as well as the surrounding facts of its publication. Though my deadline loomed, I couldn't ignore this information. I started back researching.

As I've mentioned, other than a birthplace of Jamaica Plain, Massachusetts (which is now a neighborhood in Boston), as well as birth and death dates, I hadn't been able to find any trail for Margaretta Matilda Odell. (I don't consider undocumented hearsay to be what the kids call "receipts.") On the other hand, there is plenty of information on B. B. Thatcher.

The son of Samuel Thatcher and Sarah Brown Thatcher, Benjamin Bussey Thatcher was born in Warren, Maine, in 1809 and graduated from Bowdoin College in 1826, at the age of seventeen.[45] Soon, Benjamin moved to Boston, began practicing law, and started publishing poetry and essays; his creative work appeared in *Godey's Lady's Book* in 1839 and 1840. In addition to his biography of Phillis Wheatley Peters, Thatcher published two books on Native Americans (albeit filled with unfortunate stereotypes): *Indian Biography; or, An Historical Account of Those Individuals Who Have Been Distinguished Among the North American Natives as Orators, Warriors, Statesmen, and Other Remarkable Characters*, and *Indian Traits, Being Sketches of the Manners, Customs and Characters of the North American Natives*. And he published *Memoir of S. Osgood Wright, Late Missionary to Liberia* in 1834, which appeared from George W. Light's publishing house in 1835.

In Boston, Thatcher was an anti-slavery activist. He joined the American Colonization Society, which was against slavery, but distinguished itself from the abolitionist movement in that it advocated buying and freeing enslaved blacks in the United States and settling them in Africa, though most of these people were generations removed from the continent.[46] George W. Light, the publisher of both Thatcher's and Odell's versions of Phillis Wheatley's biography, later became Light & Horton—or so it appears, since the last name of "Light" remains for the publisher, as well as the same address on Cornhill. Light & Horton published William A. Alcott's periodical *The Moral Reformer and Teacher, on the Human Constitution* in 1835.

It was in the back of Alcott's publication that I found an interesting detail, a list of "Works recently published by Light & Horton." While Thatcher's biography of Phillis Wheatley Peters is attributed to him, Odell's *Memoir* does not list her as the author:

MEMOIR OF PHILLIS WHEATLEY, a Native African and a Slave. By B. B. Thatcher, Esq. Adapted to general readers and to Sabbath Schools. With a Portrait. Second Edition. 18 mo. Cloth, 20 cents . . .

MEMOIR AND POEMS OF PHILLIS WHEATLEY. Dedicated to the Friends of the Africans. *By a relative of the Mistress of Phillis.* 18 mo. Cloth, 42 cents. [Emphasis mine.][47]

We can see that the author-less *Memoir and Poems of Phillis Wheatley* is attributed to a relative of Susannah Wheatley and costs more than twice as much as Thatcher's version, which might imply that the publisher expected to make more money on a book written by someone personally connected to the Wheatleys. When I located a second edition of Thatcher's biography of S. Osgood Wright, I found nearly the same listing for both biographies of Wheatley Peters in the back matter, except the prices of both Wheatley biographies had been omitted, and the "Portrait" in Thatcher's version was upgraded with the adjective "well-executed." Again, there is no name given for the biography that twentieth and twenty-first century readers have come to associate with Odell. On digital copies of Odell's *Memoir and Poems of Phillis Wheatley*, there is no name on the actual title page, either (for instance in the copies on Google Books and the Documenting the American South website).

What we do find in Odell's biography is language that one easily might connect to the philosophy of the American Colonization Society, the argument that American blacks, even in freedom, could not live in peace in America because of oppression: "But even were the thrall of bondage broken, the hapless victim of slavery would find himself, in but too many places, we fear, fettered by prejudice—despised by the proud—insulted by the scornful."[48] Further, *Memoir and Poems of Phillis Wheatley* is dedicated to "the Friends of the Africans." There are tiny yet substantial curiosities in this dedication. For example, the biography is *not* dedicated to "the Friends of the Negroes," to which African Americans were referred in the nineteenth century. Overwhelmingly, the term "Africans" is used throughout the biography, instead of "Negroes"—again, a possible gesture to American Colonization Society ideology that blacks in America were only temporarily displaced from their African homeland(s) and should return.

How, then, did Margaretta Matilda Odell's name get attached to *Memoir and Poems of Phillis Wheatley*, if her name was not included as an author on first or second editions? One clue might be found in that editorial footnote in volume 7 of *Proceedings of the Massachusetts Historical Society*, the one that presents (third-hand) Obour's negative feelings toward John Peters. Reading further, I saw more information about the two 1834 Wheatley biographies, although the footnote's author is unclear.

> A Memoir of Phillis, without the name of the author, was published in Boston, in 1834, by George W. Light, prefixed to a new edition of the Poems. It was written by Miss Margaretta Matilda Odell, of Jamaica Plain. . . . I subsequently called Mr. Light's attention to an advertisement (at the end of the second edition of the same Memoir, published by his house, "Light & Horton," in 1835) which gives a list of the works published by them. The first book on the list is, "Memoir of Phillis Wheatley, a Native African and a Slave. By B. B. Thatcher. Adapted to general Readers and Sabbath Schools. With a well-executed Portrait. 18 mo, cloth." On the next page is advertised the "Memoir and Poems. . . . By a Relative of the Mistress of Phillis," &c. This would indicate two memoirs, one by Thatcher, separate from the Poems; and one by a descendant of Mrs. Wheatley, with the Poems. But Mr. Light still assures me, that *there was no memoir published separately from the Poems,* and that Mr. Thatcher was not the author of any memoir of Phillis published by his house. He writes to me under the date of 23d March, 1864: "As to the Memoir, I am perfectly sure *Mr. Thatcher never did more than edit the book.*" [Emphasis mine][49]

Again, I was confused, for despite this note, there *were* two different *Memoirs* about Phillis Wheatley published by George W. Light in 1834, even if one borrowed swaths of text from the other.[50] I did more checking: in the footnotes of volume 15 of *Proceedings of the Massachusetts Historical Society*, a genealogy was provided for Odell, indicating that she is "the daughter of Captain James Odell and Margaret (Marshall) Odell"[51] The footnote goes on to draw connections between Margaretta Matilda Odell and relatives of the Wheatley family; this time, there are names, but once more, there is no documentation. This same footnote dismisses B. B. Thatcher's biography of Phillis Wheatley as "written for children," though the language of the book is quite elevated for young audiences, even by nineteenth-century standards, and describes Thatcher's book as "an abridgement of Miss Odell's Memoir."

These written dismissals of Thatcher's biography of Wheatley Peters came in 1877, forty-three years after Thatcher's book was published, and thirty-seven years after his death; thus, he couldn't dispute the characterizations of his work. Odell would not publish another book; her 1834 biography of Phillis Wheatley would be her first and last. However, Thatcher would keep publishing until his death in 1840.

Reading this new (to me) research left me with many unanswered questions.

First, because of the glaring similarities between Odell's and Thatcher's biographies on Wheatley, it's obvious that one of these writers shamelessly plagiarized from the other. But which writer plagiarized? And is the plagiarism issue why George W. Light/Light & Horton left Odell's name off *Memoir and Poems of Phillis Wheatley* for three decades?

Second, who exactly was Margaretta Matilda Odell? If Thatcher did edit her book, where did Thatcher and Odell meet and strike up a literary partnership? Was she a member of the American Colonization Society?

Third, if Odell really had authored one of the Wheatley biographies *and* had family connections to the white Wheatleys, why did George W. Light wait until thirty years after publication to reveal Odell's ostensible connection to *Memoir and Poems of Phillis Wheatley*?

And fourth—honestly—this confusion about authorship made me wonder, were B. B. Thatcher and Margaretta Matilda Odell—aka *M. M. Odell*—the *same person*? Could Thatcher have adopted a female *nom de plume* in order to sell more books for a higher price? After all, as a regular contributor to *Godey's Lady's Book*, Thatcher would have been quite familiar with a writing style that would appeal to female readers. Did his publisher want to keep selling books after Thatcher's untimely death, and so made up this story about Odell, even if she was a real person, only not the person who actually had written the biography? (Hey, listen: Stranger things have gone down in the world of nineteenth-century American publishing.)

Though I suspected that, as my southern mother might say, "something in this milk ain't clean," time constraints prohibited my conducting any more research before the deadline. My poetry book deadline loomed, and I couldn't include any of the answers to these questions here.

But you better believe that I intend to keep digging.

. . . .

All these years, I had been impatient—and honestly, *angry*—about scholars' responsibility to go back and address the Wheatley Peters historical record, but I tried to be pragmatic.

Research is hard. It's time-consuming and frustrating; I knew that from personal experience. Further, there often isn't much information for scholars to go on. For example, if Odell's *Memoir and Poems of Phillis Wheatley* were to be eliminated as a primary source for Wheatley Peters's life, what else would be left to rely upon? Precious little on the domestic interior of the woman who is the mother of African American literature.

Never mind the controversial beginning line of that poem, "'Twas mercy brought me from my *Pagan* land . . ." Phillis Wheatley Peters is much more than that. She proved something to white people about us: that we could read and think and write—and damn it, we could *feel*, no matter what the racists believed. We already knew those truths about ourselves. I'm pretty positive about that, but during her time, philosophers were arranging the "nations" with Africans at the bottom, while other Europeans measured black people's skulls alongside those of orangutans to determine if the two species were kissing cousins. In the midst of these soul assaults, an African woman's poems carried the weight for black people(s) on this side of the Atlantic. As a result, Wheatley Peters—along with black soldiers and sailors who fought on the winning side of the American Revolution, black intellectuals and writers, and various individuals of African descent asserting their God-given rights of liberty—helped to sway many white Americans and Europeans that slavery was wrong.

So I waited.

For someone to write a more emotionally charged book about Phillis Wheatley Peters, one that would take into account her pre-American existence in Africa. She was a little girl when she arrived in Boston, but she did have African birth parents. Her life did not begin in America or with slavery. She had a free lineage that did not include the Wheatleys. If nothing else, a treatment of that lineage would be an appropriate and respectful introduction to this poet's life in America.

And I waited.

For someone to include a compassionate, well-fleshed depiction of John Peters, which considers how he fit into his wife's life. Perhaps I seem naïve or silly, but I wanted scholars to view Peters as a natural occurrence in the young black poet's trajectory, instead of a low-down disruption that led to her demise.

Oddly, no account that I'd read of Peters gives the most obvious, commonsense reason for why Wheatley chose him as her mate. Maybe he didn't trick her. Maybe she wasn't desperate or temporarily out of her mind. Maybe she married John Peters because they were deeply, passionately in love.

Is that explanation so ridiculous? Why *wouldn't* they love each other? American people of African descent did fall in love back then—they still do, quiet as it's kept—and, if allowed by local power structures, they legally married. Black folks did this in the midst of war, slavery, economic chaos, and post-traumatic stress at being torn from their homelands and sent over the horrific Middle Passage. I think it's logical to assume that many, many black folks fell in love with many, many other black folks. This assumption is a rational consequence of acknowledging our black humanity.

At times, when I was impatiently waiting for scholars to reexamine the complicated realities of these two people, I imagined them. No longer by their last names, but *Phillis* and *John*, because they were real to me. I wondered what their moments together might have been.

Maybe John thought Phillis was beautiful. He was drawn to her brilliance. To her delicate face, to her very dark skin, her full lips, her tight, kinky hair, to the ring in her nose that might have been an ornament she carried from across the water. (Look very closely at that engraving in her book. Use a magnifying glass and you will see the nose ring.) And maybe she thought John was handsome. He might have looked like her relatives. He and she might have shared a hankering for a place that lived only in their memories. He might have been born in America—we probably will never know—but in any case, he would have been of African heritage. And he was a literate man. They shared a love of books.

Maybe at night, when they settled down together in their rickety bed, they talked in whispers, telling each other stories of that faraway place across the water. Folktales or proverbs that had been passed down.

John possessed ambitions, the same as Phillis, and instead of stories, maybe they talked about the future, their hopes for his fledging businesses and her second book of poetry, the glories that would be accomplished by the children they wanted. Anything was possible in that time, when messages of liberty abounded.

Maybe he was a tender lover and they laughed and cried and clutched. The words they spoke after their passion were to be believed, even though they came from the mouths of black folk.

I waited many years for somebody to see Phillis and John the way I saw them. For somebody to see her African parents as more than a few brief moments that would be forgotten by their little girl. For somebody to understand that Phillis needed Obour, because black women need other black women in their lives. I waited for somebody to love Phillis as I loved her. And then, I stopped waiting. I decided it was past time. I wrote this book.

NOTES

1. This essay was previously published in earlier form in *The Fire This Time: A New Generation Speaks About Race* (New York: Scribner, 2016).

2. [Margaretta Matilda Odell?], *Memoir and Poems of Phillis Wheatley, a Native African and a Slave. Dedicated to the Friends of the Africans.* (Boston: George W. Light, 1834), 29.

3. [Odell?], 9–10.

4. [Odell?], 9.

5. [Odell?], 9.

6. [Odell?], 10.

7. [Odell?], 17.

8. Vincent Carretta, *Phillis Wheatley: Biography of a Genius in Bondage* (Athens: University of Georgia Press, 2011), 96.

9. Carretta, 97–98.

10. Phillis Wheatley to David Wooster, 18 October 1773, from "African Americans and the End of Slavery in Massachusetts: Phillis Wheatley," Massachusetts Historical Society, https://www.masshist.org/database/viewer.php?old=1&ft=End+of+Slavery &from=%2Fendofslavery%2Findex.php%3Fid%3D57&item_id=811

11. Wheatley, Phillis, Susanna Wheatley, and Sara Dunlap Jackson, "Letters of Phillis Wheatley and Susanna Wheatley," *The Journal of Negro History* 57, no. 2 (1972): 212–13.

12. Phillis Wheatley to Obour Tanner, 21 March 1774, from "African Americans and

the End of Slavery in Massachusetts: Phillis Wheatley," Massachusetts Historical Society, https://www.masshist.org/database/viewer.php?old=1&ft=End+of+Slavery & from=%2Fendofslavery%2Findex.php%3Fid%3D57&item_id=815

13. Carretta, 21–22.

14. [Odell?], 20.

15. Phillis Wheatley to Obour Tanner, 10 March 1779, from "African Americans and the End of Slavery in Massachusetts: Phillis Wheatley," Massachusetts Historical Society, https://www.masshist.org/database/viewer.php?old=1&ft=End+of+Slavery-&from=%2Fendofslavery%2Findex.php%3Fid%3D57&item_id=818

16. [Odell?], 21.

17. [Odell?], 23.

18. [Odell?], 29.

19. Thomas Jefferson, *Notes on the State of Virginia. Illustrated with a Map, Including the States of Virginia, Maryland, Delaware and Pennsylvania* (London: John Stockdale, 1787), 150.

20. Henry Louis Gates, Jr., *The Trials of Phillis Wheatley: America's First Black Poet and Her Encounters with the Founding Fathers* (New York: Basic Civitas Books, 2003), 25–29.

21. Amiri Baraka, *Home: Social Essays*, 2nd ed. (New York: Akashic Books, 2009), 124–25.

22. [Odell?], 10.

23. Carretta, 175–77.

24. Carretta, 72.

25. Herbert Aptheker, ed., *A Documentary History of The Negro People in the United States*, 2nd. ed. (New York: Citadel Press, 1969), 6–7.

26. Belinda Sutton, "Belinda Sutton's 1783 Petition (full text)," Royall House and Slave Quarters, http://royallhouse.org/belinda-suttons-1783-petition-full-text/

27. Phillis Wheatley, *Complete Writings*, ed. Vincent Carretta (New York: Penguin Books, 2001), 86–88.

28. *A Volume of Records Relating to the Early History of Boston, Containing Boston Marriages from 1752 to 1809* (Boston: Municipal Printing Office, 1903), 441.

29. Carretta, 191–93

30. Carretta, 182.

31. [Odell?], 20.

32. Carretta, 193.

33. "November Meeting. Death of Lord Lyndhurst; Death of Hon. William Sturgis; Dr. Ephraim Eliot; Diary of Ezekiel Price; Letter of Count De Marbois; Phillis Wheatley; Letters of Phillis Wheatley," *Proceedings of the Massachusetts Historical Society* 7 (1863): 268n.

34. Carretta, 190.

35. Carretta, 190–94.

36. Ben Baack, "The Economics of the American Revolutionary War," on *E-H Net*, a website sponsored by the Economic History Association. https://eh.net/encyclopedia/the-economics-of-the-american-revolutionary-war-2/. See also Ben Baack,

"Forging a Nation State: The Continental Congress and the Financing of the War of American Independence," *The Economic History Review* 54, no.4 (2001): 639–56.

37. Carretta, 194.

38. Ashley Cataldo, e-mail message to author, October 23, 2015.

39. Robert C. Winthrop, Charles Deane, Charles Folsom, George S. Hillard, Oliver Wendell Holmes, and Andrew P. Peabody, "September Meeting. Death of George Livermore; Letter of John Wilkes; Phillis Wheatley," *Proceedings of the Massachusetts Historical Society* 8 (1864): 461–62.

40. Carretta, 194.

41. "Slavery: Slavery FAQs–Property," in *Thomas Jefferson's Monticello*, https://www.monticello.org/slavery/slavery-faqs/property/

42. "November Meeting . . . ," *Proceedings of the Massachusetts Historical Society* 7 (1863): 268n.

43. Ibid.

44. Phillis Wheatley, *The Poems of Phillis Wheatley*, ed. Julian Mason (University of North Carolina Press, 1989), 25.

45. James Grant Wilson and John Fiske, eds., *Appleton's Cyclopedia of American Biography*, vol. 6 (New York: D. Appleton and Co., 1889), 6:70–71.

46. *The Eighteenth Annual Report of the American Society for Colonizing the People of Color of The United States with the Proceedings of the Annual meeting, January 19, 1835, with a General Index to the Annual Reports and Proceedings at the Annual Meetings of the Society from the First to the Eighteenth, Both Inclusive* (Washington, 1835), 1, 5–9.

47. William A. Alcott, back matter to *The Moral Reformer and Teacher on the Human Constitution*, vol. 1, (Boston: Light & Horton, 1835–1836).

48. [Odell?], 7.

49. "November Meeting . . . ," *Proceedings of the Massachusetts Historical Society* 7 (1863): 268n.

50. Charles Deane, vice-president of the Massachusetts Historical Society, owned a copy of B. B. Thatcher's version of *Memoir*: upon Deane's death in 1898, a copy of Thatcher's *Memoir* was located in Deane's private library. See *Catalogue of the Valuable Private Library of the Late Charles Deane, L.L. D, Historian, Vice-President of the Massachusetts Historical Society and Many other Historical Societies* (Boston: C. F. Libbie, 1898), 351.

51. Robert C. Winthrop, et al. "December Meeting, 1877. Letter of Mr. Theodore Dwight; Extracts from Journal of C. J. Stratford; Signers of Declaration of Independence; Washington Benevolent Association." *Proceedings of the Massachusetts Historical Society* 15 (1876–1877): 390n.

ACKNOWLEDGMENTS

Grateful acknowledgment to the journals and anthologies in which these poems
appeared, some in earlier forms with altered titles:

Academy of American Poets website: "chorus of the mothers-griotte" and "Portrait
of Dido Elizabeth Belle Lindsay . . ."

Bearden's Odyssey: Poets Respond to the Work of Romare Bearden (TriQuarterly Books,
2017): "Blues: Odysseus"

Black Renaissance Noire: "An Issue of Mercy #1," "For the First of Several Times,
Belinda Sutton, Former Enslaved Servant of the House of Isaac Royall . . . ,"
"Homegoing . . ."

Cavalier Literary Couture: "the beautiful and the sublime"

Common-Place: The Journal of Early American Life: "Blues: Harpsichord,
or, Boston Massacre," "How Phillis Wheatley Might Have Obtained the
Approval . . . ," "Illustration: Stowage of the British Slave Ship 'Brookes' Under
the Regulated Slave Trade, Act of 1788," "Letter #16," "Lost Letter #1," "point
of no return," "Smallpox Decimates the Ranks of Lord Dunmore's Ethiopian
Regiment," and "The Transatlantic Progress of Sugar in the Eighteenth
Century"

Freeman's Family: "Lost Letter #7" and "Lost Letter #8"

The Langston Hughes Review: "Isabell"

North American Review: "Before the Taking of Goonay"

Poetry Salzburg Review: "The Death of Former President George Washington"

The Rumpus: "According to the Testimony to the Grand Jury of Newport, Rhode
Island . . ."

*What God is Honored Here? An Anthology on Miscarriage and Infant Loss by and
for Native Women and Women of Color* (University of Minnesota Press, 2019):
"Susannah Wheatley Tends to Phillis in Her Asthmatic Suffering"

First, as always, I give unashamed glory and praise to my mighty good God,
and to my Ancestors for bringing me through the painful yet ecstatic fifteen
years that it took to write this book.

Fifteen years is a long time. Plus, I'm black, and we black people always seem to
have the longest list of folks who held (and continue to hold) us down. Other
than my Creator and the Ancestors, here is why this book exists:

Thank you to my mother, Dr. Trellie Lee James Jeffers, and my father, Professor Lance Flippin Jeffers, for teaching me that in the beginning, there was the word, and the word lived in and with our black people.

Thank you to African American women poets, the mothers-griotte who continue to lead the way for me: Margaret Walker Alexander, Gwendolyn Brooks, Lucille Clifton, Jayne Cortez, Rita Dove, Mari Evans, Nikki Giovanni, June Jordan, Delores Kendrick, Sonia Sanchez, Alice Walker, and Sherley Anne Williams—and though she did not claim poetry, Toni Morrison.

Several institutions offered me precious financial assistance, time and, sometimes, space during the writing of this book: the American Antiquarian Society, the Vermont Studio Center, the National Endowment for the Arts, the Witter Bynner Foundation through the Library of Congress, the Harper Lee Awards Committee through the Alabama Writers Forum, and the University of Oklahoma.

In addition, I am incredibly grateful for the assistance of the kind and helpful research staffs at the American Antiquarian Society, Bowdoin College archives, Dartmouth College archives, Massachusetts Historical Society, Newport Historical Society, Phillips Library at the Peabody Essex Museum Library, Rhode Island Historical Society, and National Archives at Boston.

I entered the thick of this project at the American Antiquarian Society, now a sacred place for me. I would not have had the confidence to write this book were it not for the wisdom, counsel, encouragement, and patience of the great Caroline Sloat, my AAS mentor. Boundless thanks to Elizabeth Watts Pope, Curator of Books, and Ashley Cataldo, Assistant Curator of Manuscripts, who always know the answers to my questions. The continual support of my fellowship advisor (and now, AAS Director) James "Jim" Moran has been gratifying. The folks in my "too-live crew," the July 2009 fellows at the American Antiquarian Society are my biggest fans: (former AAS director) Paul Erickson, Tanya Mears, Meredith Neuman, Emily Pawley, and Jonathan Senchyne. I love y'all strong.

Other editors, poets, writers, professors, scholars, librarians, and various, wonderful human beings encouraged me while I was writing this book: Barbara Soloski Albin, Elizabeth Alexander, Julie Buckner Armstrong, Jabari

Asim, Herman Beavers, Katherine Belden, Hester Blum, Jennifer Brady, Joan Brannon, Joanna Brooks, Cyrus Cassells, Grace Cavalieri, Daniel Cottom, Ana Mae Duane, Oscar Enriquez, Ralph Eubanks, Jonathan Beecher Field, Brigitte Fielder, Nikky Finney, Ernesto Fuentes, Logan Garrison, Maryemma Graham, Rigoberto González, Lisa Gordis, Thomas Hallock, Donna Akiba Sullivan Harper, Betty Harris, Trudier Harris, Bailey Hoffner, Allison Joseph, A. Van Jordan, Catherine Kelly, Keegan Long-Wheeler, E. Ethelbert Miller, Caroline Moseley, Deborah Murphy, Mark Anthony Neal, Jon Peede, Cherise Pollard, D. A. Powell, Melynda Price, Guthrie Ramsey, Riché Richardson, Wendy Raphael Roberts, Tracy K. Smith, John Stewart, Robert Strong, Jeanie Thompson, Natasha Trethewey, Jon Tribble, Margaret Porter Troupe, Quincy Troupe, Brian Turner, Jesmyn Ward, Anthony Walton, Stephanie Powell Watts, Kathleen Welch, Cornel West, Nazera Sadiq Wright, and Hilary Wyss.

A special thank you to brothers-colleague—the "trois frères"—Chris Abani, Kwame Dawes, and Matthew Shenoda, who have enriched my understanding of and sensitivity toward African culture(s) and African poetry/poetics immeasurably.

My literary agent Sarah Burnes has been a creative muse; a wise, affectionate counselor; and a steadying force for thirteen years. Sarah, I cannot tell you how grateful I am for you.

Thank you to Julia Eagleton for her superlative competence and bolstering enthusiasm while reading this manuscript. I appreciate you so much.

Thank you to the folks at Wesleyan University Press for embracing my vision, especially Suzanna Tamminen, Stephanie Prieto, and Jaclyn Wilson. It is a joy to publish this book with you.

I have been sustained by mentors through the years. I would not be where I am without those who "stood in the gap" throughout the years: Maggie Anderson, Lucille Clifton (again), Hank Lazer, David Lynn, Jerry Ward Jr., and Afaa M. Weaver.

Thank you to "dear-dears" for constant encouragement: Remica Bingham-Risher, Andrew Jeon, Andrea Frankowiak, Mungu Sanchez, Jacqueline Allen Trimble, and Crystal Wilkinson.

Valerie Moore is the sister I found in a needful, grieving time: Girl, I love you so.

Though Miss Lucille, James William Richardson Jr. (aka "Big Poppa"), and Sidonie Colette Jeffers (aka "Sisi") have passed on to the Ancestors, they are not forgotten. I hear and feel your love on this plane, and I'm doing my best to make it to Heaven one day and help y'all consume all the hot dogs, macaroni and cheese, and sweet and sour pork we can handle.

Finally, I give gratitude for Mrs. Phillis Wheatley Peters. I lift up her genius, her sacrifice, and her courageous testimony, for she made my life as a black woman writer possible. Miss Phillis, this book is finished, but this is not the last gift I will place on your altar. My love for and devotion to you are unending. I will continue to let the people know.

NOTES ON THE POEMS

....

Most sources will be briefly identified here. For additional information about contemporary excerpts not found here, see the Bibliography that follows.

"An Issue of Mercy #1" is dedicated to Emily Pawley. The phrase *a genius child* within this poem and others is taken from Langston Hughes's poem of the same title. My poem was written after I read the biography of Phillis Wheatley Peters attributed to Margaretta Matilda Odell, but before the bulk of my archival research had begun.

"Book: Before": The poems in this section are based upon my speculation that the African child renamed Phillis was of Muslim faith, and of the Wolof people in the West African region that was called "Senegambia." In a poem that appears after her only book is published, Wheatley mentions that she was from "the Gambia." The words "yaay," "baay," and "goonay" mean, respectively, "mother," "father," and "child" in the Wolof language.

"mothering #1" is dedicated to Crystal Wilkinson.

"Fathering #1" is dedicated to Jonathan Senchyne.

"Dafa Rafet" uses a quote from Charlie Erickson—"I know all the things" —and is dedicated to him as well. "Dafa Rafet" means "It is beautiful" in Wolof.

"An Issue of Mercy #2" is written after June Jordan's "The Difficult Miracle of Black Poetry in America: Something Like a Sonnet for Phillis Wheatley."

"Book: Passage": The epigraph quotes an extant letter from Timothy Fitch to Captain Peter Gwin, found online at the Medford Historical Society website.

"Blues: Odysseus" is written after Romare Bearden's painting "Odysseus Rescued by Sea Nymphs," and "Catalog: Water" is written after N. NourbeSe Phillip's book-length *Zong!* Both of these poems reference *The Zong* slave ship massacre of 1781.

"Mothering #2": There is no documentation for which slave ship carried the child who would be renamed Phillis Wheatley, but historians have assumed that she arrived on the brig *Phillis*, because of the coincidence of her name, and the timing of the *Phillis* anchoring in Boston harbor in 1761. Further, data from the Transatlantic Slave Trade database and correspondence between Timothy Fitch and Peter Gwin identify that Gwin purchased trafficked human beings on what was known as "the Windward Coast" of Africa, which some scholars have described as the area from "Senegambia" and southeast to what is now Liberia and Cote d'Ivoire.

"Desk of Mary Wheatley . . ." is dedicated to Elizabeth Watts Pope.

"Phillis Wheatley Peruses Volumes . . ." is dedicated to Nazera Sadiq Wright.

All of the "Lost Letter" poems are written after Robert Hayden's "A Letter from Phillis Wheatley, London 1773." "Lost letter #2" and "Lost Letter #3": The latter poem is dedicated to Joanna Brooks. Selena Hastings, Countess of Huntingdon, was a key figure in the first Great Awakening, a Transatlantic spiritual movement that focused on evangelicalism. Her devotees and members of "the Huntington Connexion" included the charismatic minister Reverend George Whitefield and the Native American minister Samson Occom. Phillis Wheatley wrote and published a poem in honor of Whitfield. Susannah Wheatley corresponded with and admired the Countess of Huntington, and was a good friend of Occom. These two poems are based upon an actual "lost letter" that Phillis Wheatley wrote Occom in 1766, when he was in England on a preaching and fundraising tour for an Indian Charity School.

"Susannah Wheatley Tends to the Child Named Phillis . . ." is dedicated to Shannon Gibney.

"Lost Letter #4," "Lost Letter #5," and "Lost Letter #6": Mary Wheatley married the Reverend John Lathrop on January 30, 1771. John Lathrop was a protégé of Eleazar Wheelock, a white minister who mentored Samson Occom and directed Occom to raise funds for Indian Charity Schools founded by Wheelock, first in Connecticut, then in New Hampshire. John taught for several years at the school in Connecticut. Occom raised twelve thousand pounds for Moor's Indian Charity School, which would be around $400,000 in today's U.S. currency. Wheelock accepted Occom's money, but then reneged on his promises to build a school for Native Americans, which led Occom to openly express feelings of betrayal and outrage. Wheelock used the funds raised by Occom to start another educational institution— this time for white males; that institution is now Dartmouth College, which remains a majority white institution.

"Illustration: Petrus Camper's Measurement . . .": is written after Elizabeth Alexander's "The Venus Hottentot."

"Portrait of Dido Elizabeth Belle Lindsay . . ." and "Three Cases Decided by William Murray": Dido Lindsay was the child of William Murray's nephew and an African woman whose name is not identified in the extant historical record. She was raised within the house of William Murray, who issued the celebrated *Somerset* ruling of 1772, which made it unlawful for slaves to be forcibly taken from England and resold into slavery. As a result of this case, James Somerset went free. William Murray also decided on the outcome of both slavery insurance cases involving *The Zong* massacre of enslaved Africans.

"Found Poem: Racism" takes an excerpt from Thomas Jefferson's *Notes on the State of Virginia*.

"Phillis Wheatley is Baptized at Old South Church . . .": In this poem, the end word of each line is taken from Gwendolyn Brooks's "The Preacher Ruminates: Behind His Sermon." The poem is written according to Terrance Hayes's invented poetic form, "The Golden Shovel."

"Lost Letter #7" and "Lost Letter #8": These poems about the beginning of Phillis Wheatley's friendship with Obour Tanner are based upon my own speculation. It is not known where the two initially met.

"Thomas Wooldridge Demands that Phillis Wheatley Instantly . . ." is dedicated to Jacqueline Allen Trimble. Wheatley would later meet Wooldridges's friend the Earl of Dartmouth in 1773, when she traveled to England.

"How Phillis Wheatley Might Have Obtained the Approval . . ." and "Lost Letter #9": Henry Louis Gates Jr.'s written assertion that Wheatley met with and was interrogated by eighteen prominent white male citizens of Boston on October 8, 1772, has attained reverential status in African American literary and academic circles. Thus, it was necessary for me to render Gates's research artistically in "How Phillis Wheatley . . ." However, Joanna Brooks has offered another possible scenario of how Wheatley attained the signatures, and this informs "Lost Letter #10." Brooks writes that "the only known dated copy of the attestation appears in an advertisement in *Lloyd's Evening Post and British Chronicle* in September 1773, where it is dated 28 October 1772. Evidence shows that the attestation was signed not on or before 8 October 1772 (as Gates had asserted), but on 28 October 1772." Further, Brooks found documentation that on October 28, 1772, there was a meeting across town in Boston, making it impossible for any lengthy examination of Wheatley to have taken place on that date. Brooks argues that the "Attestation" in the front of Wheatley's book, which includes the signatures of the seventeen prominent white men of Boston as well as John Wheatley, likely was composed personally by Phillis Wheatley.

"Susannah and Phillis Wheatley Arrive at the Home of Ruth Barrell Andrews . . .": Much has been written about the dissemination of Phillis

Wheatley's poetry among well-known white Bostonians. Scholar Wendy Raphael Roberts has documented that Wheatley's poems had influence on her white contemporaries as well, such as the poet Ruth Barrell Andrews. In addition to her involvement in white female literary communities in Boston, Andrews was the wife of merchant John Andrews, whose letters in December 1773 to his brother-in-law described what would become known as the Boston Tea Party.

"Muses: Convening": The epigraphs for this part include an excerpt from Belinda Sutton's "Petition" of February 14, 1783, which is from a full manuscript found online at the Royall House and Slave Quarters website. The excerpt from the interview with Ona Maria Judge is from a manuscript found online at Encyclopedia Virginia: Virginia Humanities.

"Blues: Yemoja" is written after Audre Lorde's "From the House of Yemanjá."

"chorus of the mothers-griotte" is written after "mulberry fields" by Lucille Clifton.

"Isabell": The first recorded intact African family in seventeenth-century Virginia were three enslaved servants of one Captain William Tucker: Antoney, Isabell, and "William theire Child Baptised."

"Definitions of Hagar Blackmore" is written after A. Van Jordan's "Afterglow." A copy of the charge of Hagar Blackmore against John Manning for rape, dated April 15, 1669, was listed among "gifts to the society" in the *Massachusetts Historical Society Proceedings* in 1917.

"The Replevin of Elizabeth Freeman . . ." is dedicated to Sidonie Colette Jeffers. According to the Massachusetts Historical Society's online archives, Elizabeth Freeman and a man known as Brom enlisted a lawyer to file a writ of replevin demanding the "return of property." After the ensuing court case, both Freeman and Brom were freed.

"The Journey of Ona Judge, Enslaved Servant . . .": Ona Judge was not the only enslaved servant of George and Martha Washington who ran away, but her masters did go to extreme lengths to recapture her, including sending agents north to try to convince her to come back "home" to Mount Vernon. Judge refused and remained free until her death. In 1845, she was interviewed in the *Granite Freeman* about her experiences during slavery.

"For the First of Several Times . . ." was written after Lucille Clifton's "mulberry fields" and after Rita Dove's "Belinda's Petition" as well. Isaac Royall, Belinda Sutton's master and a loyalist to the British, made a statement in his will that he would either gift Sutton to his daughter or, if Sutton chose freedom, he would provide a legacy of thirty pounds. Royall died in 1781. Two years later, Sutton petitioned the Massachusetts General Court—the legislative body—to provide her and her differently abled daughter Prine with that pension from Royall's estate. Sutton received one payment, but then payments stopped. She continued to petition, but the payments were spotty at best. Scholars have noted that Sutton's petition is the first request by an African American for reparations, though Sutton did not asked for recompense for slavery, but rather for what had been promised her by her former master.

"Book: Voyage": The epigraph excerpt from Wheatley's letter to David Wooster is from a full manuscript found online at the Massachusetts Historical Society.

"Phillis Wheatley Embarks from Boston . . . ," "Phillis Wheatley Walks beside Her Master's Son, Nathaniel, on the Streets of London," "Ravenous Wolves in the Tower of London," and "Lost Letter #11": The first poem is written after Kevin Young's "A Farewel to America" (which was originally published as "Homage to Phillis Wheatley"). Phillis and Nathaniel Wheatley sailed from Boston Harbor on May 8, 1773, and arrived in London, England, around June 17, 1773. While there, she promoted her book of poetry. Although she would not meet the Countess of Huntingdon, to whom her book was dedicated, Wheatley did meet with Benjamin Franklin and made the acquaintance of John Thornton, with whom she would later correspond. Though correspondence by Franklin indicated that his meeting with Wheatley was less than satisfactory (in his estimation), her second poetry manuscript was dedicated to him.

"Lost Letter #14" and "Lost Letter #15": Both poems are dedicated to Tanya Mears. It is not known how Wheatley met John Peters, but there is a reference to a "young man" who was "complaisant and agreable" in an October 8, 1773, letter to Obour Tanner.

"Lost Letter #16" is dedicated to Caroline Sloat. Susannah Wheatley died on March 3, 1774.

"Lost Letter #17" and "Lost Letter #18": In an actual (extant) letter to John Thornton dated October 30, 1774, Wheatley responds to his previous suggestions for her marriage prospects to African missionaries, either John Quamine, who was free, or Bristol Yamma, who was enslaved. Samson Occom was a friend of Thornton's, too, and they may have corresponded over their concerns about Wheatley's unmarried status. Occom's fears of possible actions of Nathaniel Wheatley are speculation on my part, but we do know (from Vincent Carretta's biography) that Nathaniel had returned with his English wife to Boston on September 22, 1774. In addition, in a letter to John Thornton (dated March 29, 1774) written after Susannah Wheatley's death, Phillis Wheatley seems to suggest that her former mistress had misgivings over Nathaniel Wheatley, since he had been "an Object of so many prayers" of his mother.

"Fragment #1: First Draft of an Extant Letter . . ." uses short passages from one of Wheatley's actual letters to John Thornton, which are located in Scotland. I did not examine Wheatley's letters to John Thornton in person, but rather read them in Vincent Carretta's edited *Complete Writings* of Phillis Wheatley.

"Free Negro Courtship #2" is written after Nikki Giovanni's "Nikki Rosa."

"Lost Letter #19" and "Lost Letter #20": In his biography, Carretta writes that Wheatley probably had relocated with Mary Wheatley Lathrop and her husband John Lathrop to Providence, Rhode Island, because of the British occupation of Boston from 1775 to 1776.

"Catalog: Revolution": This entire sequence is written after Natasha Trethewey's "Native Guard" sonnet cycle. The first section epigraph is from a letter published in *The Massachusetts Gazette, and the Boston Post-Boy and Advertiser*. The second section epigraph can be found at the Founders Online website of the National Archives.

"Blues: Harpsichord . . ." is dedicated to Cherise Pollard.

"Felix . . ." is dedicated to Ashley Cataldo.

"Fragment #2: First Draft of an Extant Letter, Abigail Adams . . .": This poem is dedicated to Meredith Neuman. On September 22, 1774, Abigail Adams actually wrote to her husband in Philadelphia, where he was in residence of the First Continental Congress; in that letter, she mentions a "Conspiracy of Negroes," which may have been referring to two separate petitions by black men in 1774 that, like Felix's "Petition," asked for/demanded the freedom of all slaves in the Massachusetts colony. This poem uses short passages of Abigail's letter.

"Salem Poor Fights at the Battle of Bunker Hill": Fourteen white officers who had fought alongside this African American man at the Battle of Bunker Hill affirmed Salem Poor's bravery in a signed petition to the General Court of Massachusetts, asserting that he "behaved like an Experienced officer, as Well as an Excellent Soldier."

"Fragment #3: First Draft of an Extant Letter, Phillis Wheatley, Providence, to General George Washington . . .": Despite some suppositions that Wheatley met with Washington, at this writing there is no confirmed documentation that such a meeting ever took place, though the two did correspond. This poem uses short passages from Wheatley's actual letter to Washington.

"Lord Dunmore Decides to Offer Freedom to Slaves . . .": John Murray, Fourth Earl of Dunmore, was the British colonial governor of Virginia. His November 7, 1775, proclamation offering freedom to enslaved African American men in exchange for enlistment disturbed slaveholders of the Virginia colony, including Washington. Scholar Gary Nash has tabulated that at least five thousand black men fought on the American side of the Revolution, but perhaps as many as five to ten times that number—between 25,000 and 50,000—fought for the British.

"Smallpox Decimates the Ranks of Lord Dunmore's Ethiopian Regiment . . .": After Dunmore's Proclamation, an estimated eight hundred enslaved black men joined Dunmore's Ethiopian Regiment. The army camped close to Portsmouth, Virginia, and soon smallpox infected the entire group. The italicized portions of the poem are taken from *Report of the Record Commissioners of the City of Boston, Containing the Town Records, 1770–1777*.

"An Issue of Mercy #3": Salem Poor not only fought at the Battle of Bunker Hill, but also served in the Valley Forge encampment, alongside at least five hundred other African American soldiers.

"Harry Washington . . .": Harry Washington first ran on July 29, 1771. He was recovered the first time, but his second escape to the British forces was successful. He is recorded in British General Carlton's *Book of Negroes*, a record of African Americans emigrating to Nova Scotia from the American colonies. Harry Washington, listed as "Stout Fellow" and "formerly the property of General Washington," sailed from New York to Nova Scotia aboard *L'Abondence* on July 31, 1783.

"The Death of Former President George Washington" is written after Robert Hayden's "Those Winter Sundays." On July 9, 1799, Washington made a final will, instructing that his slaves be freed after his death, with the provision that they would not actually go free until Martha Washington died. However, a year after he passed away, his still-living wife legally freed his slaves on January 1, 1801; she died the following year.

"revolution: black sortie, black redoublé" is written after Nikki Giovanni's "The True Import of Present Dialogue, Black vs. Negro (For Peppe, Who Will Ultimately Judge Our Efforts)."

"Book: Liberty": The epigraph excerpts a letter from Wheatley to Obour Tanner that is found in a manuscript available online at the Massachusetts Historical Society website.

"Lost Letter #21": John Wheatley died on March 12, 1778. His will does not
mention Phillis Wheatley; this implies that she had been freed earlier, which
means that Nathaniel (or Mary) Wheatley had no legal claim to Phillis, and
that she wasn't in danger of being re-enslaved after John Wheatley's death.
Further, through a reading of the will, we can interpret that there might
have been ongoing tension between Nathaniel Wheatley and his father: John
Wheatley appointed his daughter's husband John Lathrop as the executor
of the will. John Wheatley left the bulk of his estate to his daughter; and he
left only twenty shillings to his son. Also, language in the will implies that
Nathaniel Wheatley had mismanaged the Wheatley family business.

"Still Life with God #2": Mary Wheatley Lathrop died on September 24, 1778.
This poem is a "Bop," a poetic form invented by Afaa M. Weaver.

"After Living Together for Several Months . . .": This poem is written after
Lucille Clifton's "if I stand in my window." In an Old South Church record,
Wheatley's marriage to John Peters is listed as April 1, 1778. However,
according to Vincent Carretta, they lived together before their marriage and
actually were married on November 26, 1778, by Reverend John Lathrop,
Mary Wheatley Lathrop's widower.

"Lost Letter #22" and "Lost Letter #23": The friction in these poems between
Obour Tanner and Phillis Wheatley Peters over John Peters is based purely
upon my own imagination. The extant correspondence between the two
friends ends in 1779. Records provided to me by Bertram Lippincott III,
librarian and genealogist at the Newport (Rhode Island) Historical Society,
indicate that on November 4, 1790, Reverend Samuel Hopkins married
Obour Tanner and one Barra (or Barry) Collins. Barra passed away on June
7, 1807, leaving his wife a house. Obour Tanner Collins passed away on June
21, 1835.

"Searching for Years but Failing to Find . . .": As of this writing, there is no
proof that Phillis Wheatley Peters ever gave birth to three children, other
than undocumented hearsay. For example, there have been no baptismal or
burial records located for any children borne by her.

"Lost Letter #24," "Lost Letter #25," and "Homegoing . . .": These three
poems are based upon my own speculation that John Peters was in debtor's
prison when Phillis Wheatley Peters passed away on December 5, 1784.
According to a timeline provided by Vincent Carretta, John Peters was
in and out of debtors' prison before and after his wife's death, but the
documentation does not tell us how long he was imprisoned during each
of his stints. Thus, Peters may have been in prison when his wife passed

away, or he might not have been. In his biography, Carretta speculates that Peters was indeed imprisoned when his wife died. At this writing, the gravesite of Phillis Wheatley Peters has not been located. John Peters died on June 2, 1801.

BIBLIOGRAPHY

MANUSCRIPT SOURCES
American Antiquarian Society
Special Collections & Archives, Bowdoin College Library
Dartmouth College Library
Massachusetts Historical Society
National Archives at Boston
The Newport Historical Society
The Phillips Library at the Peabody Essex Museum
Rhode Island Historical Society

NEWSPAPERS AND PERIODICALS
Boston-Gazette and Country Journal
Supplement to the Boston-Gazette, Etc.
Essex Gazette
Essex Journal and Merimack Packet; or, the Massachusetts and New Hampshire General Advertiser
Evening Post; and The General Advertiser
Independent Chronicle and the Universal Advertiser
Massachusetts Centinel
Massachusetts Gazette, and the Boston Post-Boy and Advertiser
Pennsylvania Magazine, or American Monthly Museum
Virginia Gazette

DATABASES AND ONLINE ARCHIVES
Accessible Archives
America's Historical Newspapers
Documenting the American South
Eighteenth Century Collections Online
Gale Primary Sources
George Washington's Mount Vernon, "Washington Library"
Internet Archive
Library of Congress Online, "Printed Ephemera Collection"
The Massachusetts Historical Society, "African Americans and The End of Slavery in Massachusetts"
The Medford Historical Society, "Slave Trade Letters"
National Archives, "Founders Online"
National Park Service, "The American Revolution: Lighting Freedom's Flame"
New England Historic Genealogical Society Database

New Yorker Online

Nova Scotia Archives, "African Nova Scotians in the Age of Slavery and Abolition: The Book of Negroes"

The Papers of George Washington Digital Edition

Royall House and Slave Quarters, "Belinda Sutton and Her Petitions"

Slave Voyages, "Trans-Atlantic Slave Trade Database," Emory Center for Digital Scholarship

Washington Post Online

BOOKS AND ARTICLES: PARTIAL LIST

Abraham, William. "The Life and Times of Anton Wilhelm Amo." *Transactions of the Historical Society of Ghana* 7 (1964): 60–81.

Adams, Abigail, and John Adams. *My Dearest Friend: Letters of Abigail and John Adams.* Edited by Margaret Hogan and C. James Taylor. Cambridge, MA: Belknap Press, 2010.

Adams, Catherine, and Elizabeth H. Peck. *Love of Freedom: Black Women in Colonial and Revolutionary New England.* New York: Oxford University Press, 2010.

Alcott, William A. *The Moral Reformer and Teacher on the Human Constitution.* Vol. 1. Boston: Light & Horton, 1835.

Archibald, Thomas H. 2017, "Washington's Runaway Slave," *Encyclopedia Virginia: Virginia Humanities*, April 21, 2017. https://www.encyclopediavirginia.org/_Washington_s_Runaway_Slave_The_Liberator_August_22_1845.

Alexander, Elizabeth. *The Venus Hottentot.* St. Paul: Graywolf Press, 2004

Aptheker, Herbert, ed. *A Documentary History of The Negro People in the United States.* 2nd. ed. New York: Citadel Press, 1969.

Baack, Ben. "The Economics of the American Revolutionary War." E-H Net, Economic History Association. https://eh.net/encyclopedia/the-economics-of-the-american-revolutionary-war-2/

———. "Forging a Nation State: The Continental Congress and the Financing of the War of American Independence." *The Economic History Review* 54, no. 4 (2001): 639–56.

Bacon, Margaret Hope. "Quakers and Colonization." *Quaker History* 95, no. 1 (Spring 2006): 26–43.

Baraka, Amiri. *Home: Social Essays.* 2nd ed. New York: Akashic Books, 2009.

Barry, Boubacar. *Senegambia and the Atlantic Slave Trade.* New York: Cambridge University Press, 1997.

Bassard, Katherine Clay. *Spiritual Interrogations: Culture, Gender and Community in Early African American Women's Writing.* Princeton: Princeton University Press, 1999.

Brace, C. Loring. *Race is a Four-Letter Word: The Genesis of the Concept.* New York: Oxford University Press, 2005.

Brice-Saddler, Michael, "The 7-Year-Old Girl Who Died in Border Patrol Custody

Was Healthy before She Arrived, Father Says," Washington Post, December 15, 2018, www.washingtonpost.com/nation/2018/12/15/year-old-girl-who-died -border-patrol-custody-was-healthy-before-she-arrived-father-says/.

Brooks, Gwendolyn. *The Essential Gwendolyn Brooks*. Edited by Elizabeth Alexander. New York: Library of America, 2005.

Brooks, Joanna. *American Lazarus: Religion and the Rise of African-American and Native American Literatures*. New York: Oxford University Press, 2003.

———. "Our Phillis, Our Selves." *American Literature* 82, no. 1 (2010): 1–28.

Burdett, Everett W. *History of the Old South Meeting-House in Boston*. Boston: B. B. Russell, 1877.

Byles, Mather. *Poems on Several Occasions*. Boston: S. Kneeland and T. Green, 1744.

Bynum, Tara. "Phillis Wheatley on Friendship." *Legacy* 31, no. 1 (2014): 42–51.

Camper, Petrus. *The Works of the Late Professor Camper on the Connexion between the Science of Anatomy and the Arts of Drawing, Painting, Statuary, Etc Etc in Two Books*. Translated by T. Cogan. London: C. Dilly in the Poultry, 1794.

Carretta, Vincent. *Phillis Wheatley: Biography of a Genius in Bondage*. Athens: University of Georgia Press, 2011.

———. "Phillis Wheatley, the Mansfield Decision of 1772 and the Choice of Identity." In *Early America Re-Explored: New Readings in Colonial, Early National, and Antebellum Culture*, edited by Claus H Schimdt and Fritz Fleischmann, 175–89. Lexington: University of Kentucky Press, 1999.

Chernow, Ron. *Washington: A Life*. New York: Penguin Group, 2010.

Chotiner, Isaac. "Q & A: Inside a Texas Building Where the Government Is Holding Immigrant Children." *New Yorker*, June 22, 2019, www.newyorker .com/news/q-and-a/inside-a-texas-building-where-the-government-is-holding -immigrant-children.

Christaller, Rev. J. G. *A Grammar of the Asante and Fante Language called Tshi [Chwee, Twi]: Based on the Akuapem Dialect with Reference to the other (Akan and Fante) Dialects*. Basel: Basel Evangelical Missionary Society, 1875.

Clifton, Lucille. *The Collected Poems of Lucille Clifton*. Edited by Michael Glaser and Kevin Young. Rochester: BOA Editions, 2012.

A Companion to Every Place of Curiosity and Entertainment in And About London and Westminster, Containing An Historical Description of London, The River Thames, The Tower of London, London-Bridge, The Monument, The Royal Exchange, The Mansion House, Guildhall, St. Paul's Cathedral, The British Museum, Westminster Abbey, Westminster-Bridge, St. James Park and Palace, The Queen's Palace, The Winter and Summer Diversions, Greenwich Hospital and Park, Kensington, Kew, and Hampton-court Palaces and Gardens, Windsor Castle, And of many other Places. 3rd ed. London: J. Drew, W. Nicoll, Messrs. Richardson and Urquhart, J. Pridden, and T. Durham, 1772.

Curtin, Philip D. *Africa Remembered: Narratives by West Africans from the Era of the Slave Trade*. Madison: University of Wisconsin Press, 2012.

Dain, Bruce. *A Hideous Monster of the Mind: American Race Theory in the Early Republic*. Cambridge: Harvard University Press, 2002.

Deane, Charles. *Catalogue of the Valuable Private Library of the Late Charles Deane, L.L. D., Historian, Vice-President of the Massachusetts Historical Society and Many other Historical Societies.* Boston: C. F. Libbie, 1898.

DeWolf, Thomas Norman. *Inheriting the Trade: A Northern Family Confronts Its Legacy as the Largest Slave-Trading Dynasty in History.* Boston: Beacon Press, 2008.

Diouff, Sylviane. *Servants of Allah: African Muslims Enslaved in the Americas.* 15th ed. New York: New York University Press, 2013.

Dunbar, Erica Armstrong. *Never Caught: The Washingtons' Relentless Pursuit of Their Runaway Slave, Ona Judge.* New York: Atria / 37 Ink Books, 2017.

Dunbar, Paul Laurence. *Majors and Minors: Poems.* Toledo: Hadley & Hadley, 1895.

Dove, Rita. *Collected Poems: 1974–2004.* New York: W. W. Norton, 2017.

Dow, George Francis. *Slave Ships and Slaving.* Salem: Marine Research Society, 1927.

Egerton, Douglas R. *Death or Liberty: African Americans and Revolutionary America.* New York: Oxford University Press, 2009.

The Eighteenth Annual Report of the American Society for Colonizing the Free People of Color of The United States with the Proceedings of the Annual meeting, January 19, 1835, with a General Index to the Annual Reports and Proceedings at the Annual Meetings of the Society from the First to the Eighteenth, Both Inclusive (Washington, 1835).

Eze, Emmanuel Chukwudi, ed. *Race and the Enlightenment: A Reader.* Oxford, UK: Blackwell Publishing, 1997.

Fenn, Elizabeth A. *Pox Americana: The Great Smallpox Epidemic of 1775–82.* New York: Hill and Wang, 2001.

Fisher, Linford D. *The Indian Great Awakening: Religion and the Shaping of Native Cultures in America.* New York: Oxford University Press, 2012.

Gamble, David. *The Wolof of Senegambia, Together with Notes on the Lebu and the Serer.* London: International African Institute, 1957.

Gates, Henry Louis, Jr. "Editor's Introduction: Writing 'Race' and the Difference It Makes." *Critical Inquiry* 12 (1985): 1–20.

———. *The Trials of Phillis Wheatley: America's First Black Poet and Her Encounter with the Founding Fathers.* New York: Basic Civitas Books, 2003.

Giovanni, Nikki. *The Collected Poetry of Nikki Giovanni, 1968–1998.* New York: Harper Perennial, 2007.

Greene, Lorenzo J. "Mutiny on the Slave Ships." *Phylon* 5, no. 4 (1944): 346–54.

Hale, Thomas A. "Griottes: Female Voices from West Africa." *Research in African Literatures* 25, no. 3 (1994): 71–91.

Harding, Alan. *The Countess of Huntingdon's Connexion: A Sect in Action in Eighteenth-Century England.* New York: Oxford University Press, 2003.

Harris, Will. "Phillis Wheatley, Diasporic Subjectivity, and the African American Canon." *MELUS* 33, no. 3 (2008): 27–43.

Hill, Hamilton Andrews. *History of the Old South Church (Third Church) Boston, 1669–1884.* Vol. 2. Boston: Houghton, Mifflin and Company, 1890.

Hoare, Prince. *Memoirs of Granville Sharp, Esq., Composed from His Own Manuscripts, and Other Authentic Documents in the Possession of His Family and of the African Institution.* London: Henry Colburn, 1820.

Homer. *The Odyssey.* Translated by Robert Fagles. New York: Penguin Classics, 1999.

Hopkins, Samuel. *The Works of Samuel Hopkins, D.D. First pastor of the Church in Great Barrington, Mass., Afterward Pastor of the First Congregational Church in Newport, R.I., with A Memoir of his Life and Character.* Vol. 1. Boston: Doctrinal Tract and Book Society, 1854.

Hotten, John Camden, ed. *The Original Lists of Persons of Quality; Emigrants; religious exiles; political rebels; serving men sold for a term of years; apprentices; children stolen; maidens pressed; and others who went from Great Britain to the American Plantations, 1600–1700: with their ages and the names of the ships in which they embarked, and other interesting particulars; from mss. preserved in the State Paper Department of Her Majesty's Public Record Office, England.* London: John Camden Hotten, 1874.

Hughes, Langston. *The Collected Poems of Langston Hughes.* Edited by Arnold Rampersad and David Roessel. New York: Vintage Classics, 1995.

Huntington, Reverend E. B. *A Genealogical Memoir of the Lo-Lathrop Family in this Country, Embracing the Descendants as far as Known.* Ridgefield: Mrs. Julia M. Huntingdon, 1844.

Hutchinson, Thomas. *The Diary and Letters of His Excellency Thomas Hutchinson, Esq, Captain-General and Governor in Chief of his Late Majesty's Province of Massachusetts Bay in North America.* Edited by Peter Orlando Hutchinson. Vol. 2. Boston: Houghton & Mifflin.

Isani, Muktar Ali. "Contemporaneous Reception of Phillis Wheatley: Newspaper and Magazine Notices During the Years of Fame: 1765–1774." *Journal of Negro History* 85, no. 4 (2000): 160–73.

Jeffers, Honorée Fanonne. "'The Dear Pledges of Our Love': A Defense of Phillis Wheatley's Husband." In *The Fire This Time: A New Generation Speaks About Race,* edited by Jesmyn Ward, 62–83. New York: Scribner, 2016.

———. "Phillis Wheatley's Word," *Commonplace: the journal of early American life,* http://commonplace.online/article/the-age-of-phillis/.

Jefferson, Thomas. *Notes on the State of Virginia. Illustrated with a Map, Including the States of Virginia, Maryland, Delaware and Pennsylvania.* London: John Stockdale, 1787.

Johnson, Cynthia Mestad. *James DeWolf and the Rhode Island Slave Trade.* Charleston: The History Press, 2014.

Jones, Adam and Marion Johnson. "Slaves from the Windward Coast." *The Journal of African History* 21, no. 1 (1980): 17–34.

Jordan, A. Van. *M-A-C-N-O-L-I-A.* New York: W. W. Norton, 2004.

Jordan, June. *Some of Us Did Not Die: New and Selected Essays of June Jordan.* New York: Basic Civitas Books, 2002.

Kachun, Mitch. "From Forgotten Founder to Indispensable Icon: Crispus Attucks,

Black Citizenship, and Collective Memory, 1770–1865." *Journal of the Early Republic* 29, no. 2 (2009): 249–86.

Kant, Immanuel. *Essays and Treatises on Moral, Political, Religious and Various Philosophical Subjects. From the German by the Translator of the Principles of Critical Philosophy. In Two Volumes.* Vol. 2. London: Printed for the Translator, 1799.

Kerber, Linda K. *Women of the Republic: Intellect and Ideology in Revolutionary America.* Chapel Hill: University of North Carolina Press, 1980.

Killick, David. "Invention and Innovation in African Iron-smelting Technologies." *Cambridge Archaeological Journal* 25, no. 1 (2015) 307–19.

Lathrop, John. *Discourse at Boston on the Death of Mrs. Mary Lathrop, his wife, who died September 24, 1778.* Boston, 1779.

Lorde, Audre. *The Collected Poems of Audre Lorde.* New York: W. W. Norton, 1997.

Lovejoy, Paul E., and Carolyn A. Brown. *Repercussions of the Atlantic Slave Trade: The Interior of the Bight of Biafra and the African Diaspora.* Lawrenceville: Africa World Press, 2011.

May, Cedrick. *Evangelism and Resistance in the Black Atlantic, 1760–1835.* Athens: University of Georgia Press, 2008.

McBride, Dwight. *Impossible Witnesses: Truth, Abolitionism, and Slave Testimony.* New York: New York University Press, 2001.

McCullough, David. *1776.* New York: Simon and Schuster, 2005.

Midgley, Clare. "Slave Sugar Boycotts, Female Activism and the Domestic Base of British Anti-Slavery Culture." *Slavery and Abolition* 17, no. 3 (1996): 137–62.

Mustakeem, Sowandé. "'She must go overboard & shall go overboard': Diseased Bodies and the Spectacle of Murder at Sea." *Atlantic Studies* 8, no. 3 (2011): 301–16.

Nash, Gary B. *The Forgotten Fifth: African Americans in the Age of Revolution.* Cambridge: Harvard University Press, 2006.

———. *The Unknown American Revolution: The Unruly Birth of Democracy and the Struggle to Create America.* New York: Penguin Books, 2005.

"November Meeting. Death of Lord Lyndhurst; Death of Hon. William Sturgis; Dr. Ephraim Eliot; Diary of Ezekiel Price; Letter of Count De Marbois; Phillis Wheatley; Letters of Phillis Wheatley." *Proceedings of the Massachusetts Historical Society* 7 (1863): 168–279.

Occom, Samson. *The Collected Writings of Samson Occom, Mohegan: Leadership and Literature in Eighteenth-Century Native America.* Edited by Joanna Brooks. New York: Oxford University Press, 2006.

[Odell, Margaretta Matilda?]. *Memoir and Poems of Phillis Wheatley, a Native African and a Slave. Dedicated to the Friends of the Africans.* Boston: George W. Light, 1834.

Oldham, James. *English Common Law in the Age of Mansfield.* Chapel Hill: University of North Carolina Press, 2004.

———. "Insurance Litigation Involving *The Zong* and Other British Slave Ships, 1780–1787." *The Journal of Legal History* 28, no. 3 (2007) 299–318.

Osumare, Halifu. *The Hiplife of Ghana: West African Indigenization of Hip Hop.* London: Palgrave Macmillan, 2012.

Otero, Solimar, and Toyin Falola, editors. *Yemoja: Gender, Sexuality, and Creativity in the Latina/o and Afro-Atlantic Diasporas.* Albany: SUNY Press, 2013.

Pettigrew, William A. *Freedom's Debt: The Royal African Company and the Politics of the Atlantic Slave Trade.* Chapel Hill: University of North Carolina Press, 2013.

Philip, N. NourbeSe. *Zong!* Middletown: Wesleyan University Press, 2011.

Pope, Alexander, *Complete Poetical Works.* Edited by Henry Walcott Boynton. Boston: Houghton Mifflin, 1903.

Rediker, Marcus. *The Slave Ship: A Human History.* New York: Penguin Group, 2008.

Report of the Record Commissioners of the City of Boston, Containing Boston Births from A.D. 1700 to A.D. 1800. Boston: Rockwell and Churchill, 1894.

Report of the Record Commissioners of the City of Boston, Containing the Town Records, 1770–1777. Boston: Rockwell and Churchill, 1887.

Rhodehamel, John, editor. *The American Revolution: Writings from the War of Independence.* New York: Library of America, 2001.

Richardson, David. "Shipboard Revolts, African Authority, and the Atlantic Slave Trade." *The William and Mary Quarterly* 58, no. 1 (2001): 69–92.

Roberts, Wendy Raphael. "'Slavery' and 'To Mrs. Eliot on the Death of Her Child': Two New Manuscript Poems Connected to Phillis Wheatley by the Bostonian Poet Ruth Barrell Andrews." *Early American Literature* 51, no. 3 (2016): 665–81.

Robinson, William H. *Critical Essays on Phillis Wheatley.* Boston: G. K. Hall & Co, 1982.

———. *Phillis Wheatley: A Bio-Bibliography.* Boston: G. K. Hall & Co, 1981.

———. *Phillis Wheatley in the Black American Beginnings.* Detroit: Broadside Press, 1975.

Shields, John C. "Phillis Wheatley and Mather Byles: A Study in Literary Relationship." *CLA Journal* 23, no. 4 (1980): 377–90.

———. *Phillis Wheatley and the Romantics.* Knoxville: University of Tennessee Press, 2010.

———. *Phillis Wheatley's Poetics of Liberation: Background and Contexts.* Knoxville: University of Tennessee Press, 2008.

———. "Phillis Wheatley's Use of Classicism." *American Literature* 51, no. 1 (1980): 97–111.

Shields, John C., and Eric D. Lamore, eds. *New Essays on Phillis Wheatley.* Knoxville: University of Tennessee Press, 2011.

Smith, Justin E. H. *Nature, Human Nature, and Human Difference: Race in Early Modern Philosophy.* Princeton: Princeton University Press, 2015.

Stanwood, Edward. "October Meeting, 1916. Gifts to the Society; Thomas Russell Sullivan; Letters of John Stuart Mill, 1865–1870; Letter of Elkanah Lane, 1839; George Harris Monroe." *Proceedings of the Massachusetts Historical Society* 50 (1916): 1–36. http://www.jstor.org/stable/25080056.

Thatcher, B. B. *Indian Biography; or, An Historical Account of Those Individuals*

Who Have Been Distinguished Among the North American Natives as Orators, Warriors, Statesmen, and Other Remarkable Characters. 2 vols. New York: J & J Harper, 1832.

———. *Indian Traits, Being Sketches of the Manners, Customs and Characters of the North American Natives.* 2 vols. New York: Harper and Brothers, 1840.

———. *Memoir of Phillis Wheatley, a Native African and a Slave.* Boston: George W. Light, 1834.

———. *Memoir of Rev. S. Osgood Wright, Late Missionary to Liberia.* 2nd ed. Boston: Light & Horton, 1835.

———. "Religious Character of the Poetry of Mrs. Heman." *Godey's Lady's Book, and Ladies American Magazine* 20–21 (October 1840): 165–69.

———. "Sketches of English Ladies. The Queen." *The Lady's Book.* 18–19 (February 1839): 87–91.

———. "To a Consumptive." *The Lady's Book.* 18–19 (October 1839): 168.

Trethewey, Natasha. *Native Guard.* New York: Houghton Mifflin, 2007.

Vansina, Jan. "Linguistic Evidence for the Introduction of Ironworking into Bantu Speaking Africa." *History in Africa* 33 (2006): 321–61.

Vermulen, Han F. *Before Boas: The Genesis of Ethnography and Ethnology in the German Enlightenment.* Lincoln: University of Nebraska Press, 2015.

A Volume of Records Relating to the Early History of Boston, Containing Boston Marriages from 1752 to 1809. Boston: Municipal Printing Office, 1903.

Walker, Margaret. *On Being Female, Black and Free: Essays by Margaret Walker, 1932–1992.* Edited by Maryemma Graham. Knoxville: University of Tennessee Press, 1997.

Walvin, James. *The Zong: A Massacre, the Law, and the End of Slavery.* New Haven: Yale University Press, 2011.

Weincek, Henry. *An Imperfect God: George Washington, His Slaves, and the Creation of America.* New York: Farrar, Straus and Giroux, 2003.

Wheatley, Phillis. *Complete Writings.* Edited by Vincent Carretta. New York: Penguin Books, 2001.

———. *Phillis Wheatley and Her Writings.* Edited by William H. Robinson. New York: Garland Publishing, 1984.

———. *The Poems of Phillis Wheatley.* Edited by Julian Mason. Rev. ed. Chapel Hill: University of North Carolina Press, 1989.

———. *Poems on Various Subjects, Religious and Moral.* London: A. Bell, 1773.

Wheatley, Phillis, Susanna Wheatley, and Sara Dunlap Jackson. "Letters of Phillis Wheatley and Susanna Wheatley." *The Journal of Negro History* 57, no. 2 (1972): 211–15.

Wilson, James Grant, and John Fiske, eds. *Appleton's Cyclopedia of American Biography.* Vol 6. New York: D. Appleton and Co., 1889.

Winthrop, Robert C., et al. "September Meeting. Death of George Livermore; Letter of John Wilkes; Phillis Wheatley." *Proceedings of the Massachusetts Historical Society* 8 (1864): 442–62.

Winthrop, Robert C., Ellis Ames, and R. C. Waterston. "December Meeting, 1877. Letter of Mr. Theodore Dwight; Extracts from Journal of C. J. Stratford; Signers of Declaration of Independence; Washington Benevolent Association." *Proceedings of the Massachusetts Historical Society* 15 (1876): 386–404.

Young, Kevin. *Blue Laws: Selected and Uncollected Poems, 1995–2015.* New York: Alfred A. Knopf, 2016.

ABOUT THE AUTHOR

Honorée Fanonne Jeffers is the author of the novel *The Love Songs of W.E.B. Du Bois* and four previous books of poetry: *The Gospel of Barbecue* (Kent State, 2000), *Outlandish Blues* (Wesleyan, 2003), *Red Clay Suite* (Southern Illinois, 2007), and *The Glory Gets* (Wesleyan, 2015). Individual poems have appeared in *American Poetry Review*, *Gettysburg Review*, *Iowa Review*, *Prairie Schooner*, and *Angles of Ascent: A Norton Anthology of Contemporary African American Poetry*, among many other journals and anthologies. For her poetry, she has been awarded fellowships from the American Antiquarian Society, the Bread Loaf Writers Conference, the National Endowment for the Arts, the Rona Jaffe Foundation, the Vermont Studio Center, and the Witter Bynner Foundation through the Library of Congress.

A prose writer as well as poet, her essays and fiction stories have appeared in the journals *Black Renaissance Noire*, *Callaloo*, *Common-Place: The Journal of Early American Life*, *Indiana Review*, *JENda: A Journal of Cultural and African Studies*, *The Kenyon Review*, *New England Review*, *StoryQuarterly*, *Virginia Quarterly Review*, and in the book *The Fire This Time: A New Generation Speaks on Race*. For her fiction, she has won the Emerging Fiction Fellowship from the Aspen Summer Words Conference, the Tennessee Williams Scholarship in Fiction from the Sewanee Writers' Conference, and the Goodheart Prize for Fiction from *Shenandoah: The Washington and Lee University Review*. Her cultural criticism blog *PhillisRemastered* has had more than a quarter of a million visits.

In 2018, Honorée Fanonne Jeffers was given the Harper Lee Award as Alabama's Distinguished Writer of the Year, which recognizes lifetime achievement. She is a professor of English at the University of Oklahoma.